Hans Christian
ANDERSEN

Hans Christian ANDERSEN

The Misunderstood Storyteller

Jack Zipes

Routledge
Taylor & Francis Group
NEW YORK AND LONDON

Published in 2005 by
Routledge
Taylor & Francis Group
270 Madison Avenue
New York, NY 10016

Published in Great Britain by
Routledge
Taylor & Francis Group
2 Park Square
Milton Park, Abingdon
Oxon OX14 4RN

Printed in the United States of America on acid-free paper
10 9 8 7 6 5 4 3 2 1

International Standard Book Number-10: 0-415-97432-1 (Hardcover) 0-415-97433-X (Softcover)
International Standard Book Number-13: 978-0-415-97432-5 (Hardcover) 978-0-415-97433-2 (Softcover)

Library of Congress Cataloging-in-Publication Data

Catalog record is available from the Library of Congress

Taylor & Francis Group
is the Academic Division of T&F Informa plc.

Visit the Taylor & Francis Web site at
http://www.taylorandfrancis.com

and the Routledge Web site at
http://www.routledge-ny.com

HANS CHRISTIAN ANDERSEN, THE DANISH ROMANCE-WRITER.

For Klaus Doderer
In honor of his 80th birthday

Contents

Illustrations

Cover: Hans Christian Andersen, oil painting by C. A. Jensen, 1836.

Frontispiece: Hans Christian Andersen, The Danish Romance Writer, from Hans Christian Andersen. *The Fairy Tale of My Life.* London: Paddington Press, 1871.

1. Hans Christian Andersen. *The Little Mermaid and Other Stories.* Trans. R. Nisbet Bain. Illustr. J. R. Weguelin. London: Lawrence and Bullen, 1893.

   Naughty Boy — p. 83
   The Little Mermaid — p. 117

2. *Hans Andersen's Fairy Tales.* Trans. Carl Siewers. Illustr. Joseph J. Mora. Boston: Dana Estes, 1887.

   The Tinderbox — p. 33
   The Traveling Companion — p. 61
   The Little Match Girl — p. 90
   Bronze Pig — p. 93
   The Snow Queen — p. 97
   The Little Mermaid — p. 111
   The Swineherd — p. 124
   Emperor's New Clothes — p. 128

3. *Hans Christian Andersen's Fairy Tales.* Illustr. W. Heath Robinson. London: Hodder & Stoughton, 1900.

   The Nightingale — p. 38

Preface

No other notable European writer did more to make himself misunderstood by his readers while begging for their recognition than Hans Christian Andersen. Not that any writer can ever be fully understood the way he or she wants to be grasped. Part of all great writing is its elusiveness, and a writer, especially a writer of fairy tales, purposely wants to elude his readers. Andersen knew this, but he wanted to become famous and recognized as a great writer exactly because he was so elusive. He wanted to be admired not as a writer for children, but as a genial artist who commanded all forms of writing — poetry, drama, novels, essays, librettos, travel books, short stories, and fairy tales. He wanted to bask in divine glory, for he believed that God had assigned him a special place on earth. Yet, today he is known primarily as a writer of fairy tales for children, perhaps one of the most original and gifted, and in English-speaking countries, even this recognition is somewhat limited and distorted by images and representations of Andersen and his tales in popular culture.

Certainly we shall never learn who the "true" Hans Christian Andersen was or what the "truths" of his works are. But we may learn more about him and appreciate his accomplishments by discovering who he was not and by critically reappraising all his works. It is only through a socio-historical critique that we can reflect upon his contemporary significance. Such an approach to Andersen and his writings is not meant to diminish his significance, especially as a writer of fairy tales. Rather, it is more an endeavor to reappraise his stature during the commemoration of his 200th birthday. It seems to me to be more appropriate not to sing his praises and join the fanfare of celebration that might further the misrecognition about which he complained, but to take him seriously and xiv • Hans Christian Andersen

evaluate what exactly it was and is in his writings that has appealed to millions of readers, young and old, throughout the world.

My focus in this short study is on Andersen's production of fairy tales and his relevance as a fairy-tale writer. Outside of Denmark, his fame rests on his fairy tales and on a very limited number of his tales. Few people realize that he wrote 156 tales and stories, and that the majority of them were intended more for adults than for children. Few people realize that Andersen had a very tenuous relationship with children, and that he led a very troubled life. One need only read his diaries and letters to realize that he was a pathetic individual, pathetic in the sense that he excited pity and compassion from other people because he was so desperate to be loved and praised and to take his place among the elite in Europe, if not in Heaven. As early as 1837, when he was still forging his career, Andersen wrote:

> My life is really a poetic story, surely I am a poet! The son of the poor washerwoman running around in the streets of Odense in his wooden shoes has already come so far that he is treated like a son in the home of one of Denmark's most estimated men and has friends among honorable and wonderful people. One has to mention me as one of the good writers of my time, but I want even more! God granting me sufficient strength, I want to be mentioned among Denmark's best writers together with Heiberg and Oehlenschläger! But there is one more leap to take, a great leap upwards. I really sense it, although I don't like to talk about it. The good Lord must take me by the arm; it's no use just lifting my legs. But cheer up! A great writer here and a greater one still in the next world, that is the image of my hopes, and it is a bad soldier who doesn't think of becoming a general, as the proverb says.[1]

What makes Andersen so fascinating as a person and writer is not so much his self-infatuation and vanity, but that he concealed as much as he revealed in his behavior and works. The veil of concealment was thin, however, and it is painful to read the hurt and rage in his tales that account for their profound dramatic tension. One must indeed be careful not to read Andersen too much into his tales and other works. Yet, to a certain extent, it is somewhat unavoidable: he embodies his thoughts and desires in his writings, and there is a great temptation to read the fairy tales as autobiographical representations. This would, however, be doing him a disservice. The ugly duckling may resemble Andersen and the course of his life up to 1843, but the young swan mistaken for a duckling is not Andersen. His life was not a fairy tale, and he did not become an elegant white swan. He never escaped his impoverished childhood but carried it with him throughout his life and fought his demons through his works, which represent more than what Andersen was and wanted to be. The strong moral and idealistic components in Andersen's tales illustrate the values and the type of "proper" behavior that were needed to survive in the society of his times. His tales are projections from his own experiences that he wanted to convey to his readers, for he implicitly wanted them to avoid the pitfalls and misery that he knew only too well. His tales are also theoretical speculations about the nature and beauty of art and the qualities a great artist needs to gain the recognition he deserves. His tales are often didactic, sentimental, and religious, for Andersen was a God-fearing, superstitious, and anxious writer who sought to quell sexual urges that disturbed him. His art was a form of control and often a genre of revenge through which he gained the just rewards that he felt had been denied him.

Over thirty years ago I began studying and writing about Andersen and his fairy tales, and during the course of this time, I published two essays that sought to explore the unusual dynamics in his works. These essays form the basis of two chapters in my present study, "In Pursuit of Fame" and "Discourse of the Dominated," and since I have changed some of my ideas and altered the focus of my critique, I have thoroughly revised and expanded these essays for this book, and I have benefited from the most recent scholarships on Andersen such as Jens Andersen's excellent biography, *Andersen–En Biografi* (2003), which I read in German. The other two chapters, "The Discourse of Rage and Revenge" and "The Cinematic Appropriation of Andersen's Heritage: Trivialization and Innovation," are entirely new and deal with aspects of Andersen's fairy tales that have received scant attention. Andersen had very little contact with children in his adult life, and his attitude toward children reflected very conservative Christian principles, which might explain why Andersen's fairy tales were so widely accepted by the middle classes, especially in England and America. In fact, the Danish scholar Viggo Hjørnager Pedersen has argued that "Andersen is to all intents and purposes an English writer, read by millions of people who do not understand a word of Danish, and exerting more influence on English children's writing than any native Briton until Lewis Carroll."[2] Andersen's tales have clearly an international appeal and have been adapted and appropriated by different writers and filmmakers over the years. This is why I have included a lengthy chapter about the film adaptations of Andersen's tales in America and Europe. There is now the "American" Andersen as well as a French, Russian, Czechoslovakian, and so on, and his image and the significance of his works are conveyed through the medium of film. Most famous, of course, is the Disney interpretation of Andersen, an approach that trivializes his works to such an extent that one must wonder if it hasn't caused Andersen to turn over in his grave. Indeed, he might not even recognize his very own work.

This brings us full circle to the "misunderstood" storyteller. There are many cultural and individual understandings and misunderstandings of Andersen's life and fairy tales. Our present understanding of Andersen's life and fairy tales in the twenty-first century has been enriched by the efforts of critics and artists to explain the meaning of his life and works. My own critique is intended as a modest but provocative contribution to the scholarship on Andersen with the hope that I may cause some eyebrows to be raised while revealing some new aspects of this pathetically great artist.

Acknowledgments

I would like to thank Poul Houe for his thorough reading of my manuscript and for all the wise and helpful suggestions and corrections he made. In addition, Marte Hult provided a great deal of sound advice and questions that made me rethink my interpretations. As usual, Bill Germano was the driving force behind my work. There are few editors in the publishing industry as gracious and effective as Bill, who took extra time to make this book possible. In the New York office of Routledge, Fred Veith was most helpful in organizing and preparing my manuscript for the initial copyediting process, and Tao Woolfe at the Boca Raton office of Taylor & Francis did careful work as project editor overseeing the book in its final stages. Finally, I can never thank my wife, Carol Dines, enough for her strong support and encouragement.

In Pursuit of Fame:
An Introduction to the Life and
Works of Hans Christian Andersen

Hans Christian Andersen spent his life pursuing fame. In this respect the famous fairy-tale writer was a crazed lover, obsessed by fame. At a very early age he declared himself willing to suffer all kinds of humiliation and denigration to fulfill what he felt to be his divine destiny, to be a writer. Egocentric to the core, persistent, and patient, he denied himself so that destiny would not be denied.

Andersen's perseverance was astounding. Yet his narcissistic striving to succeed as a great writer was also profoundly sad. The strain he placed himself under to produce was so great that he often succumbed to bouts of hypochondria, melancholy, and depression. His nerves became like volatile wires, frayed and tattered. By the time he finally forced fame to turn and smile on him, he was a lonely and desperate man. Not only did he question whether he was worthy of fame, but he demanded even more admiration and applause than he had already gained. He licked the boots of the aristocracy to obtain support, and he complained when the Danish nation did not continually crown his head with laurels. He perfected his dress and manners to conceal his desperation. He undertook numerous trips abroad to seek peace of mind. But he could not escape the fact that his life had become an aborted fairy tale and that fame had a Medusa's head.

Whenever he took pen in hand, it was to shield himself from his fears and to vent his anger. His fairy tales were of the life he did not lead, and they spoke what he wanted to say publicly but did not dare. His writings were majestic acts of self-affirmation and self-deception. They did indeed bring him fame, and he did indeed become one of the most famous writers of his day, as he had hoped; but they also prevented the world from knowing him. Even today, the world-famous Hans Christian Andersen is really unknown.[1]

The public image of Hans Christian Andersen still prevalent is one fed by the lies and myths he created. For instance, most of the photographs and portraits of Andersen reveal a man at ease with himself, a gentle, composed man sometimes telling stories benevolently to children. He is always well dressed and appears in poses of perfect propriety. He is tall, gaunt, and not particularly handsome. Like the photographers and painters, most biographers have contributed to the deception of the public by emphasizing the quaint and gentle composure of the imaginative writer. They have associated him with the ugly duckling and sketched his life as the poor, gifted son of a cobbler who transformed himself into a successful, "beautiful" writer through his magical, innate talents: Hans Christian Andersen as fairy tale. His name has become virtually synonymous with the genre.

Yet to see him and his work as fairy tale is to do him an injustice. Andersen wrote over thirty plays, six novels, three autobiographies, and several travel books and volumes of poetry, aside from numerous essays, tales, and stories. He was respected and revered during his lifetime as an avant-garde writer. A gifted orator and performer, he felt at home in all social classes, was one of the most widely traveled men of letters in Europe, and made the personal acquaintance of most of the prominent authors of the nineteenth century. These features of his life and work tend to be forgotten or neglected. The fame of the fairy tales has dwarfed both his total artistic achievement and his pathetic personal history.

One of the difficulties in writing about Andersen as Denmark's most versatile and famous writer is that he himself wrote three autobiographies, all of which tend to distort facts. His first attempt to document his life was *H. C. Andersens Levnedsbog* 1805–1831, written in 1832. It was not discovered until 1926, when it was published in Danish. His second endeavor, *Das Märchen meines Lebens ohne Dichtung*, completed in 1847, was published first in German and English as *The True Story of My Life*. The third account, *Mit Livs Eventyr* (1855), was translated as *The Fairy Tale of My Life* in 1868; this title indicates how Andersen continually sought to portray himself in all his autobiographical writings as a type of romantic hero, a poor swineherd turned into a prince. For instance, the 1847 version begins as follows:

My life is a beautiful fairy tale, rich and glorious. If I had gone out into the world as a poor and lonely boy and had met a powerful fairy, and if she had said, "Choose your own course and goal in life, then I shall protect and lead you according to the development of your mind and the way things must reasonably happen in this world," then my destiny could not have been happier, nor more cleverly or better guided than the case has been. The story of my life will tell the world what it has told me: there is a loving God who directs everything for the best.

In 1805 there was a newly married couple, a cobbler and his wife, who lived in a small impoverished room in Odense. They loved each other dearly and deeply. He had just turned twenty-two, a remarkably talented man with a genuine poetic nature. She was somewhat older, ignorant about things concerning the world and life, but kind and generous. The man had recently become a guild master and had built his own shoemaker shop and wedding bed. For this purpose he had used the wooden frame on which the coffin of the dead Count Trampe had recently rested. The shreds of the black sheet, which were always to be found on the bed frame later, were souvenirs of this event. Then, on April 2, 1805, instead of the count's corpse, there was a live, crying child on this bed surrounded by flowers and candelabras. That was me, Hans Christian Andersen.[2]

About the only thing true here is the date of Andersen's birth. The fact is that nobody knows exactly where Andersen was born. His parents had been married only two months before his birth and had no permanent residence. His father, Hans Andersen, who was born in 1782, became a journeyman shoemaker. In other words, he belonged to the lowest class of artisans and barely made enough to support himself and his family. He liked to read, take walks in the countryside, and make toys for his son. This was his talented or poetic side. Otherwise, he was known to be a skeptical thinker, inclined to doubt the tenets of traditional Christianity. He died in 1816 after a desperate attempt to make money for the family by enlisting as a soldier in Napoleon's army.

Andersen's mother, Anne Marie Andersdatter, was born in 1775 and worked as a servant in various houses in Odense. In 1799 she gave birth to an illegitimate daughter. Later, after Andersen was born, she worked as a laundress and took other menial jobs. Far from being ignorant of the world, she knew real social conditions only too well. When Andersen refers to her as "ignorant," he means that she was illiterate, coarse, and superstitious. Such were Andersen's parents, and the noted Andersen biographer Elias Bredsdorff paints a more accurate picture of the writer's beginnings than the writer himself when he notes:

> Andersen's background was, from a social point of view, the lowest of the low: grinding poverty, slums, immorality and promiscuity. His grandmother was a pathological liar, his grandfather insane, his mother ended by becoming an alcoholic, his aunt ran a brothel in Copenhagen, and for years he was aware that somewhere a half-sister existed who might suddenly turn up and embarrass him in his new milieu — a thought that haunted his life and dreams.[3]

Andersen's life was anything but a fairy tale. Though his parents doted on him, there was little they could offer him. Overly sensitive about his family's poverty and his own homely appearance, Andersen kept to himself. He had few friends and preferred to stay at home, where he would play with pictures, puppets, and dolls. By the time he was five, he was sent to school. His memories of this youth reveal a special fascination with the Odense jail and insane asylum, which were joined under a single roof. Given the history of insanity and immorality in his family, he feared going insane and being confined. At the same time, he was also intrigued and attracted by the strange people in the jail and asylum. But more important than this attraction was his budding love for the theater.

Odense, a tiny city of 8,000 inhabitants, boasted a municipal theater that produced comic operas, operettas, and plays. When he was seven, his parents took Andersen to the theater, and a new, fantastic world exploded before his eyes: from this point on, theater life came to represent a glorious realm of freedom from the misery of his life, and he hoped to become a great writer involved with the stage. At home, he began dressing up in costumes, acting out roles, and writing plays. As soon as he was able to read Shakespeare, he gave recitals of his own plays to anyone he could attract. His mother became upset by her son's theater mania, but her threats of punishment had no effect. And after the death of her husband in 1816, she was rarely at home to keep an eye on him. In fact she had become so poor that she sent her eleven-year-old son to work against his will. Engaged as an apprentice in a cloth mill, Andersen did not last long there. He could not bear the obscenity and rough treatment of the journeymen, and he left after he was ridiculed and manhandled during a recitation of songs for his fellow workers. His next job was in a tobacco factory, where he worked until his lungs became slightly damaged. His mother then had no choice but to allow him to remain at home, where he devoted himself once again to books and playacting. It was also during this time that Andersen began making money by singing in the homes of middle-class families and became known for his charming voice as "the little Nightingale of Funen."

In July 1818 Andersen's mother remarried. Her new husband was another journeyman cobbler, but despite his low status, the financial situation of the family improved. Andersen could now attend the local church school, where he was expected to forget theater and poetry and submit to rigorous religious training. Yet Andersen's obsession with the theater was stronger than the school's discipline. Upon his confirmation, in 1819, he was willing to risk anything for a chance to pursue his calling as an artist, although his mother tried to convince him to learn a trade. Finally, knowing how superstitious his mother was, Andersen persuaded her to visit a fortuneteller, who predicted that her son would achieve fame in the world. For Andersen, the world meant Copenhagen, and in the fall of 1819 the fourteen-year-old Andersen set out for the city.

Copenhagen destroyed many of his illusions, and the period 1819–1822 was one of trial and hardship. At that time the capital was a relatively small port city of 120,000 inhabitants, and Danish society, dominated by the aristocracy and upper-middle classes, was highly stratified. Though there were increasing signs of liberalism and possibilities for social advancement as Denmark underwent a gradual transition from late feudal absolutism to a form of constitutional monarchy that only took hold in the 1840s, the king and his close advisers played an enormous role in all decisions pertaining to government, economy, and the arts. Most of the leading writers of the day, such as Adam Oehlenschläger and Johan Ludvig Heiberg, were dependent on patronage. Almost all the major cultural institutions, such as the theater, ballet, opera, and symphony, benefited from royal subsidies and private contributions. It was practically impossible for a member of the lower classes to establish himself socially, for success did not require "genius" as much as manners, breeding, formal training, and connections. Andersen had none of these. Instead, he was helped by the fact that he was naive and foolhardy, entirely unaware that he was pursuing the impossible.

Certainly he was not prepared for the Copenhagen he encountered in 1819. He arrived during vicious anti-Semitic riots that raged for more than ten days, and rented a tiny room in a poor district of the city. He then experienced a series of setbacks that almost caused him to return to Odense. Armed with a letter of introduction to the famous ballerina Anna Margrethe Schall at the Royal Theater, he made the first of numerous attempts to impress important people with his talent. During his first interview he took off his shoes to demonstrate how well he could dance. Given his awkwardness, this was a catastrophic sally, and he was obliged to leave as soon as he could find his shoes. Similar catastrophes followed; soon he began to feel that he would find neither employers nor patrons to back his artistic career. Yet Andersen's determination and unusual capacity for improvisation eventually did make an impression on various philanthropic gentlemen, who collected money for him to attend ballet school and later to take singing lessons. He even appeared in some small roles at the Royal Theater. Nevertheless, despite such training and experience, Andersen was never able to cut a gracious figure onstage; and the plays and poems that he began producing were either imitative or pretentious.

This pretentiousness was evident in the way he signed his first book, *Ungdoms-Forsøg* (*Youthful Attempts*, 1822). He chose the nom de plume Villiam Christian Walter out of admiration for William Shakespeare and Sir Walter Scott, and he filled the book with stereotypes, stilted verse, and melodramatic scenes copied from his masters. Indeed, it became evident to all concerned (even to himself) that Andersen needed more formal schooling if he was to attain a measure of success as a writer or performer. Fortunately for him, the board of directors at the Royal Theater decided to offer him a three-year scholarship to attend a private school in Slagelse, a town fifty-six miles west of Copenhagen. Even more important was the choice of Jonas Collin, director of the board and a prominent legal administrator, as Andersen's prime adviser. A sober, highly intelligent, and sensitive man, Collin became Andersen's major benefactor and acted as his father for most of the writer's life. But Andersen had to endure five years of strict schooling before he was entirely accepted into the Collin home as an "adopted" son, and even then it was questionable whether he was accepted.

Although Andersen was seventeen when he entered the school at Slagelse, he had to be placed among the eleven-year-olds. This situation was humiliating for him, but he knew practically no Latin, Greek, geometry, geography, or history. Though he read voraciously, his grammar and style were faulty, and he remained an atrocious speller to the end of his life. Bothered by his deficiencies, Andersen pursued his studies with a vengeance. Despite his zeal, however, there were problems. The headmaster, Dr. Simon Meisling, was a moody, dissatisfied person who was apt to belittle the young man when he least expected it. For the next five years Andersen had to contend with Meisling's disparaging treatment in addition to the attempts of Meisling's wife to seduce him. Since he had few friends at school, he was often despondent, depending on letters and contacts from outside to encourage him in his studies. Andersen felt plagued by self-doubt and regarded the regimentation of school as stifling to a prospective writer with great imaginative powers. Meisling discouraged him from following his artistic leanings, and even Collin forbade him to write poetry for some time. Nevertheless, he was not to be deterred from pursuing his chosen destiny. In the spring of 1823 he wrote in a letter: "If anyone can become a poet [*Digter*] through the events of his childhood, then I will become one. Not a minor one, however, there are plenty of those. If I cannot become a great one, I shall strive to become a useful citizen in the community."[4]

All or nothing — this was typical of Andersen. His use of the Danish word *Digter* is significant. Like the German term *Dichter*, it implies more than just "poet": it is often used to designate a great writer. And as Andersen's diary entries testify, he yearned to be nothing more and nothing less than a *Digter*:

> What could become of me, and what will become of me? My powerful fantasy will drive me into the insane asylum, my violent temper will make a suicide of me! Before, the two of these together would have made a great writer [*Digter*]! Oh God do Your ways really prevail here on earth? — Forgive me, God; I am unfair to You who have helped me in so many ways. Oh, You are God, so forgive and go on helping me. (God, I swear by my eternal salvation never again within my heart to mistrust Your fatherly hand, if only I might this time be promoted to the fourth form and to Elsinore.)[5] (20 September 1825)

> Everything is guided by God. There is destiny. Man is free like the horse on a rocky island that can roam freely, but there are certain limits: it cannot go beyond them! You want the best for yourself by obtaining faith in yourself. So I seek my destiny, all bountiful God! — May the Lord arrange things so that good

fortune accompanies me! If it is Your will that I become a Digter, You will not weaken my courage and rob me of my talents. My soul lives only for poetry. I believe to have felt Your hand as destiny has taken its course. Do not rob me of Your faith, my Lord, my Father, my one and only. Hear your weak child![6]
(27 September 1825)

It was not God who came to the rescue, though Andersen would have liked to believe this. Rather it was Jonas Collin, who interceded on his behalf whenever he had disputes with Meisling. By 1826, after the head-master and Andersen had both been transferred to a school in Helsingør, it became clear to Collin that his sensitive ward could no longer endure Meisling's harshness. So he gave Andersen permission to move to Copenhagen to prepare for his final examinations, which he passed in 1828. The next year, Andersen recorded another success when he took his university admission tests. However, he had no intention of attending the university, for he had already drawn attention to himself as a writer. His second book, *Journey on Foot from Holmens Canal to the East Point of Amager*, written in imitation of E. T. A. Hoffmann, his literary idol at that time, was published in 1829; and his first play, *Love on St. Nicholas Tower*, was produced that same year at the Royal Theater. In 1830 a volume of poetry, *Digte* (*Poems*) appeared containing "Min Tankes Tanke ene Du er vorden" (You my thought), which Edvard Grieg later set to music. Ten years after Andersen had arrived in Copenhagen, he had begun to be noticed by high society.

From 1830 to 1835 Andersen sought to establish himself as one of the most promising, if not the most promising, writers in Denmark. He wrote plays, poems, travel books, and stories. He took trips outside Denmark to seek fresh impulses for his writing. In 1831 he journeyed to Germany, Bohemia, and Switzerland, and in each country he tried to advance his career by making the acquaintance of prominent people and leading writers of the time. In particular he was drawn to the German romantics, Ludwig Tieck in Dresden and Adalbert von Chamisso in Berlin, who was the first translator of his poems into German. In 1833 Andersen received a two-year travel grant from King Friedrich VI, and he used it to visit the major cities of France, Italy, Switzerland, and Germany. In Paris he met Victor Hugo and Heinrich Heine. In Italy he spent most of his time with the sculptor Bertel Thorvaldsen, the writer Henrik Hertz, and other Scandinavian artists. During these trips he completed another volume of poetry and the long dramatic poem *Agnete and the Merman*. He also kept a personal diary in which he often complained about sickness and melancholy, and described people, cities, and landscapes as though he were writing for posterity.

When one reads Andersen's diaries and letters, it is evident that he felt most at home outside Denmark, especially because he could not bear the negative reviews that his poems, plays, and novels received from time to time. His constant journeys gave him a sense of freedom and an opportunity to mix with extraordinary and influential people. He rarely referred to his family background and visited his mother only two or three times after leaving Odense. At the time of her death, in 1833, he was in Rome and wrote in his diary:

> Today I bought myself a brazier. It is standing on one side of me, and the sun is shining from the other. It makes me feel better, but I am somewhat debilitated. If only there were a letter for me today! — There was a letter from Collin senior; it reported my mother's death. My first reaction was: Thanks be to God! Now there is an end to her sufferings, which I haven't been able to allay. But, even so, I cannot get used to the thought that I am so utterly alone without a single person who must love because of the bond of blood! — I also received some critical commentary from Heiberg about my two singspiels — I am just an improvisator! — People are anxious about the criticism of my Agnete, and Reitzel doesn't dare risk one hundred rix dollars on it. Now I'll have to publish it myself![7] (16 December 1833)

These remarks reveal key features of narcissism and self-deception in Andersen's thinking. His diaries and letters show that he was inclined to pity himself, and it appears that his egoism prevented him from realizing a deep filial love and from experiencing either a fulfilling heterosexual or homosexual love. His chronic psychological problems stemmed largely from his incapacity to fulfill his sexual fantasies and erotic wishes, to assert himself as he wished to be understood. Andersen never married and never had sexual intercourse. For a long time, literary historians and psychologists speculated that he was homosexual, but recent scholarship such as Jens Andersen's superb biography, *Andersen–En Biografi* (2003) suggests that he never acted on his homosexual inclinations. Jackie Wullschlager makes his alleged homosexuality a central issue in her recent biography, *Hans Christian Andersen: The Life of a Storyteller*

(2000), whereas Diana Crone Frank and Jeffrey Frank in their 2003 introduction to Andersen's fairy tales take a different view:

> Since 1901, when a Danish writer using the pseudonym Albert
> Hansen broached the subject in a German magazine, researchers
> have conducted a somewhat tedious debate about whether
> Andersen was gay. But the only evidence for that comes from a
> literal reading of the often overheated language of the nineteenth
> century. As an older man, he [Andersen] was occasionally
> infatuated with men as well as with women, most notably with the
> dancer Harald Scharff, but Andersen's virginity almost certainly
> remained intact. His novels and plays, though intended for adults,
> rarely touched on desire in any form other than the standard
> literary tropes of the era — sighs, tears, and polite embraces.[8]

The question of his sexual preference is, indeed, a side issue, while
sexuality in general was a great issue in his works. He appears to have
been an emotional cripple who failed to satisfy his desires and needs in
intimate relationships of any kind. There is also a certain fear of sexual
and erotic arousal that he apparently tried to tame in his tales. Often his
tortured soul led him to torture the "innocent" characters in his stories in
clear acts of revenge. He recorded his disappointments in the women and
men of his real life in almost all his works, and he often portrayed himself
as the "victim" of unreciprocated love.

During the 1830s Andersen was attracted to three women: Riborg
Voigt, the sister of a friend; Mathilde Ørsted, the daughter of the prominent physicist Hans Christian Ørsted; and Louise Collin, the youngest
daughter of Jonas Collin. In all three instances, he avoided making a firm
proposal of marriage because he feared commitment and was uncertain
about his "manliness." His letters and diaries reveal that he felt socially
and psychologically inferior to women. Lack of money, low social origins, ugliness, shame of his mother, the need for privacy — these were
some of the factors that drove him to reject himself before he could be
rejected by women. There was a strong element of masochism in his relations with women that was also manifested in his relations with men. Jens
Andersen suggests that Andersen tended to approach women so he could
be closer to their brothers or husbands. In addition, his love for women
was coupled sometimes with a brutal misogynistic tendency that was
strangely inverted, if not perverted, so that he might be identified with

the victim. But despite his suffering, Andersen enjoyed the "romantic" role of the rejected lover, a role that was to figure prominently in almost all of his novels and many of his tales.

Aside from the tentative relationships with Riborg, Mathilde, and Louise, Andersen developed a close friendship with Henriette (Jette) Wulff, with whom he shared his most intimate thoughts. A forthright, intelligent woman and champion of revolutionary causes, Jette Wulff was the daughter of Peter Wulff, who later became an admiral and had made Andersen a welcome guest in his home during the 1820s. A semi-invalid, Jette Wulff was one of the few women who did not threaten him sexually. Andersen took her criticism and concern to heart because he felt she supported him in his endeavors and rarely flattered him without good cause. If not for her tragic death off the coast of America in 1853, Andersen might have come to the United States. It had been her dream to settle in America, and she had encouraged her friend, who often made disparaging remarks about Denmark, to think about emigration.[9]

The only other woman who figured prominently in Andersen's life as an "amour" was the famous singer Jenny Lind, who was known as the "Swedish Nightingale." He met her in 1840 and actually courted her for a short period, until it became apparent that she was not at all interested in Andersen and certainly not in a marriage with him. For Andersen, who shunned illicit relationships and brothels, his amorous feelings for Jenny Lind could be sanctified only through marriage. That he repressed his sexual drives so severely may have led to psychosomatic disturbances and may account for his extraordinary vanity. Andersen sought outlets for his repressed sexuality in masturbation (as he records in his journals) and in performing his works (perhaps subconsciously an act of public masturbation). Moreover, his writings were part of a complex process of sublimation. His creative efforts became a necessity; what he referred to as his calling was his compulsive and therapeutic need to contend with neurosis. The more Andersen denied himself, his social background, and his sexual drives, the more he felt called upon by "God" to express his sensitive "genius." But this was a mission that the great Danish philosopher Søren Kierkegaard doubted whether Andersen understood. In his critique of Andersen's novel *The Improvisatore*, he wrote in *From the Papers of One Still Living* (1838): "Genius is not a wick that's blown out by a wind, but a firestorm that only the wind challenges."[10] This was a critique that filled Andersen with dread, perhaps because it questioned his masculinity.

As was customary in those days, Andersen formed close male friendships that were marked by homoeroticism. He studied with boys, was looked after by men, traveled exclusively with male peers, moved in male-ordained social circles, and explored realms open primarily to men. It is thus no wonder that Andersen placed men on a pedestal, and glorified the male condition in a traditional, chauvinist manner. For instance, at the beginning of his novel *O. T.* (1836) he states:

> There is a condition of happiness which no poet has yet properly sung, which no lady-reader, let her be ever so amiable, has experienced or ever will experience in this world. This is a condition of happiness that alone belongs to the male sex, and even then alone to the elect.... Happy moment, which no woman, let her be ever so good, so beautiful, or intellectual, can experience — that of becoming a student, or, to describe it by a more usual term, the passing of the first examination! The cadet who becomes an officer, the scholar who becomes an academic burgher, the apprentice who becomes a journeyman, all know, in a greater or less degree, this loosening of the wings, this bounding over the limits of maturity into the lists of philosophy.[11]

Whereas he feared women and gave voice to his fear by rejecting them or getting them to reject him, he felt more free to express his love for men — albeit a masochistic love — in letters and in conversation. His lifelong friendship with Edvard Collin is perhaps the best example of the kind of amorous relationship he had with men. The eldest son of Jonas Collin, somewhat younger than Andersen, Edvard Collin became the legal administrator who managed Andersen's literary and business affairs. Though Collin, like Jette Wulff, was critical of Andersen's melodramatic, egocentric tendencies and fierce ambition, he remained a devoted friend and adviser.

At one time he hurt Andersen deeply by refusing to address him with the familiar "you," or du in Danish, and he reprimanded him often because of the writer's excessive public displays, which went against the Lutheran grain of this prudent Danish bureaucrat. But Andersen desired and actually needed to establish a master-servant relationship with Collin. At the same time, he honestly complained that the two of them were not on equal terms. He wanted to have it both ways. Generally speaking, Andersen placed himself in Collin's control by seeking his approval for everything he wrote and by putting his business affairs in his hands. Whenever Collin became severe or critical, Andersen would play the role of the spurned servant-lover, feeling comfortable and productive in this situation. He re-created it time and again in other male relationships. Whether in quest of male or female love, Andersen generally adopted the obsequious attitude that suited his neurotic temperament. It was through portraying this dubious social and psychological situation in his writings that he achieved a measure of stability. In his best fairy tales, he used humor effectively to question his rigidity and reconcile his contradictory drives. But in many of his longer narratives, he would often take himself too seriously and expose his feelings of inferiority through sentimentality and religiosity.

By the early 1830s, Andersen had drawn attention to himself in Copenhagen as a gifted writer, but it was not until 1835 that he achieved a major breakthrough and tasted fame. Upon returning from Italy he published his novel *Improvisatoren* (*The Improvisatore*, 1835), the first Danish experimental novel of social realism. At the same time, he printed four stories for children in his first slender volume of fairy tales, and with each successive volume his reputation spread throughout Europe. Actually, fame came to Andersen more slowly in Denmark than in Germany, England, and France, and he continually complained about the devastating attacks on his works by leading Danish writers. As noted above, Søren Kierkegaard wrote an entire book ridiculing *The Improvisatore*, and other writers were no less cruel, especially in their reviews of his sentimental plays. Andersen, however, was not singled out for unusual treatment; it had become fashionable for Danish critics to write with a barbed pen. Moreover, he had his fair share of good press. After publishing the novels *O. T.* and *Kun en Spillemand* (*Only a Fiddler*, 1837), two additional collections of fairy tales, and several plays, Andersen had no cause to complain, especially after King Friedrich VI granted him an annual poet's pension of 400 rix dollars for the rest of his life, a sum augmented at different times later in his career. Thus by 1838 Andersen could feel financially secure, and he was recognized by Danish royalty as one of the kingdom's finest artists.

Unfortunately, he never felt emotionally secure. In Copenhagen his vanity was so well known that he became an easy target for criticism, some of it justified, some of it malicious. Andersen was like a child who cannot control his urge to be the center of attraction. He continually baffled himself and others because he could not restrain his urge to act out his eccentricities in public. For example, he seized every opportunity to recite his poems and stories in public. Once, in Rome, he intruded on a dinner party in a small restaurant and insisted on reading "The Ugly Duckling" to a group of people he barely knew. When they politely suggested that he might enjoy himself more by sightseeing than by reading stories in a restaurant, he answered that he would prefer to entertain them in this way. Then, without further ado, he pulled a manuscript from his pocket and read.

This incident is not meant to imply that he was always overbearing. On the contrary, he tried to conceal his ambitious and competitive nature with his will to please and his desire to perform. Georg Brandes, the renowned Danish literary critic, remarked astutely of the writer:

> Indeed, he did become a great man. But he did not become a man. There was not the slightest glimmer of manliness in the soul of this child, son of the common people. Much later he developed self-confidence. He developed it from the praise he received abroad but never manly vigor and courage. He lacked an aggressive spirit entirely, nor did he have the means to take the offensive. Never in his life did it occur to him to attack a powerful person for a good cause. He himself had been a poor devil much too long and needed love, kindness, goodwill, and especially recognition. If he used a weapon, then it was for self-defense and always in poetic form: his pen had a blunted point.[12]

Heinrich Teschner recorded Heinrich Heine's perceptive appraisal of Andersen's character:

> He seemed to me like a tailor. This is the way he really looks. He is a haggard man with a hollow, sunken face, and his demeanor betrays an anxious, devout type of behavior that kings love. This is also why they give Andersen such a brilliant reception. He is the perfect representation of all poets just the way kings want them to be.[13]

Andersen as child and tailor. This childlike "tailor" was to impress the Western world with his talents from 1840 to 1875. Indeed, it should be stressed that he was like a wandering tailor who put his skills to use by making fine ornaments and clothes for "emperors." Characteristic of Andersen is the fact that, even though he eventually could have afforded to establish a permanent residence in Copenhagen, he never did so. He traveled extensively almost every year and left Denmark whenever he could. Soon after the success of his play *Mulatten* (*The Mulatto*) in 1840, he embarked for Germany and Italy on his first train ride, and he wrote enthusiastically about the railroad, which added a new dimension to his view of people and the countryside. He knew he was always welcome in foreign countries, where he was wined, dined, and feted by the aristocracy, and received with honor in the best of the bourgeois homes and literary salons. In Denmark he was also given generous invitations to visit the estates of friends. Of course it was expected that Andersen would perform for his hosts and display his genius; and he did, often without their asking. Not only did he recite his work, but he was also fond of making unusual paper cuts to amuse his hosts and their children.

Andersen's rate of artistic production during this time was astounding. Between 1840 and 1850 he finished several plays, wrote the travel book *En Digters Bazar* (*A Poet's Bazaar*, 1842), published poetry, completed a novel, and edited a new volume of fairy tales practically every year. The revolutionary upheavals of 1848–50 were reflected in some of his stories, but Andersen, who basically supported the cause of enlightened monarchy, avoided direct involvement in political affairs. By 1850 he himself had become a kind of Danish institution. During the 1850s and 1860s Andersen concentrated more and more on his fairy tales, which were no longer designated for children. He also published the second version of his autobiography, produced the travel book, *In Sweden* (1851), saw Charles Dickens in England for a second time, and made a trip to Zurich, where he met Richard Wagner. Andersen appreciated Wagner's imaginative use of folklore and was one of the first writers to recognize the composer's radical attempt to transform opera into a total artwork for all classes. By 1860 Andersen's annual pension had been increased to one thousand rix dollars, and he could afford extended journeys, such as the one he took to France, Spain, and North Africa, which he recorded in travel books such as *In Spain* (1863). When the war between Denmark and Prussia broke out in 1864, he was deeply torn, especially because he had numerous friends in Germany, where he had always been prized as a great *Dichter*. In fact, the king of Prussia had presented him with his first royal medal in 1846. However, Andersen's loyalties were clearly with Denmark; he remained in Copenhagen and devoted himself to writing new plays and fairy tales. In 1866, after the war, he resumed his travels and took the opportunity to visit Paris, where he received a special decoration. In 1869 he was honored with the Commander Cross in Copenhagen.

Sensing he was coming to the end of his career, Andersen wrote another autobiographical novel, *Lykke-Peer* (*Lucky Peter*), in 1870. Even in old age, the desire to transform his youth into a fairy tale did not abate, and he remained as active as ever during the last five years of his life, making trips to Germany, Austria, Italy, and Switzerland and continuing to write tales. However, his decline between 1873 and 1875 was noticeable and marked by numerous instances of embarrassing behavior. After July of 1874 he lived in considerable isolation in his own rooms in Nyhavn and later moved to Rolighed where he was cared for by his good friend Mrs. Melchior. By the early summer of 1875 it became apparent that Andersen had cancer of the liver, yet he did not give up hope that a miracle would bring about a complete recovery. Indeed, after recuperating from an attack that had kept him bedridden, he made plans for another trip abroad. But his hopes for recovery were illusory, and he died on 4 August 1875.

Andersen's Works

In the English-speaking world, the critical evaluation and general reception of Andersen's creative works have been confined largely to his fairy tales. Yet, as we have seen, such exclusive focus on the tales has contributed to a misunderstanding of the man and a neglect of his full literary achievement. To grasp the total significance of this remarkable man — "the tailor as romantic" — he must be viewed in the context of Danish culture and the theater scene in Europe.

Denmark experienced a major cultural shift at the beginning of the nineteenth century, from the universality of classicism to the romantic cult of genius and individualism. In part this was brought about by the lectures of Henrik Steffens. He introduced the German romantic writers and philosophers to the Danish intelligentsia, in particular to Oehlenschläger and N. F. S. Grundtvig, who in turn forged new paths in the arts and education for further generations of Danish writers. As Niels Kofoed has commented:

> Whenever a new era is inaugurated in the history of literature, its activities do not restrict themselves to a limited field such as music or poetry. The new ideas penetrate all spheres of civilization with a reorganizing will. The aesthetics of romanticism were rooted in eighteenth-century philosophical debates and inquiries into art, poetry, and beauty, and Denmark with its geographically strategic position as the gateway to the North has over the years functioned as a catalyst for various trends coming from Germany, England, and France being adopted by

the other Scandinavian countries, transforming them according to national standards and capabilities. So it also happened with the romantic movement.[14]

An impressionable and voracious reader, Andersen benefited from the exciting cultural changes. He was particularly fond of German fairy-tale writers such as Ludwig Tieck, Novalis (Friedrich von Hardenberg), E. T. A. Hoffmann, Friedrich de La Motte-Fouqué, and Adalbert Chamisso. In addition, he was attracted to the writings of Jean Paul Richter, Friedrich von Schiller, and Johann Wolfgang von Goethe, and was influenced by Shakespeare, Scott, and Washington Irving. But most important for his development was the peculiar form assumed by the Danish romantic movement, which was, as W. Glyn Jones notes:

> accompanied by what is known as the Aladdin motif, after the idea which Oehlenschläger expresses in his play *Aladdin*. This deals with the theory that certain people are chosen by nature, or God, or the gods, to achieve greatness, and that nothing can succeed in stopping them, however weak and ill-suited they may otherwise seem.... The twin themes of former national greatness and of the possibility of being chosen to be great, despite all appearances, assumed a special significance for Denmark after 1814."[15]

It was Oehlenschläger who signaled the coming of the golden age of Danish literature with his poem "The Golden Horns" (1802), written after a famous encounter with Steffens. This work celebrates Denmark's pagan past and recounts how the gods took back their great gift to the Danes because greed had made them unworthy of their heritage. This national ballad, Oehlenschläger's other poems, and his drama *Aladdin* (1805) instilled a new sense of hope and confidence in Danish social leaders, who had lost Norway and political and economic power during the Napoleonic wars. To regain national pride after 1814, the aristocracy and the prosperous middle classes were more willing than ever to encourage and support creative and scientific experimentation: tiny Denmark was to show its greatness.

Aside from Oehlenschläger, numerous other talented writers and artists began to make names for themselves. Grundtvig produced significant works in the fields of theology, history, politics, and education. Bernhard Severin Ingemann glorified the Danish Middle Ages in his epic poems and novels. Hans Christian Ørsted became one of the discoverers of electromagnetics and espoused a philosophy of the immortality of the soul that was to influence Andersen. Thorvaldsen became one of the leading sculptors in Europe. C. W. Eckersberg established himself as one of the finest romantic painters in Denmark, and Steen Steensen Blicher founded the Danish short story. Not only did Andersen absorb and learn from the works of these Danish writers, artists, and intellectuals, but he also came in contact with many of them: they served as both inspiration and point of departure for his writing.

Of all the Danish writers, the great dramatist and literary critic Johan Ludvig Heiberg played an immense role in Andersen's development. Heiberg was the pioneer of vaudeville in Danish theater. More important, the caustic criticism and sharp wit of the *Kjøbenhavns flyvende Post* (*Copenhagen Flying Post*), the literary journal he edited, elevated him to the position of cultural arbiter in Copenhagen. Some of Andersen's early poems and stories were printed by Heiberg, who first encouraged and later demoralized him. With his modern ironic sensibility and training in Hegelian dialectics, Heiberg influenced and judged almost all the prominent young Danish intellectuals of his time: Kierkegaard, who began writing his great philosophical works in the 1830s and 1840s; Hertz, who became one of the leading dramatists of this period; and Hans Peter Holst, who was active as a novelist, poet, and dramatist. These three writers and others competed with Andersen for Denmark's laurels and patronage. In an era of growing individualism, when the middle classes were seeking more power in central and northern Europe; when industrialism and urbanization were bringing rapid changes in cultural life and social mobility; when revolutions were changing the maps, mentalities, and hegemonies of European nations; when Denmark was forced to open its tight-knit society slightly to outside influences, it is not surprising that Andersen felt there was also a possibility for a talented young man to establish his claim to genius. The challenge was there. Andersen was imaginative, enterprising, and ingratiating.

Andersen's versatility as a writer needs to be addressed before we discuss the significance of his fairy tales and consider how and why they have so completely overshadowed his other works in the twentieth and twenty-first centuries. Here we must bear in mind that Andersen desired to make a name for himself first as a dramatist, novelist, poet, and travel writer, not as a writer of fairy tales, and especially not as a writer for children. Although he worked with fairy-tale motifs from the beginning of his career and saw his own life as a type of fairy tale, the short narrative form was not at first his favorite means of embodying his ideas and dreams.

Andersen's greatest love was unquestionably the theater and the musical world.[16] Ever since his first visit to the Odense theater in 1812, he had dreamed of performing and writing plays. In the course of his life he composed over thirty dramatic works, and twenty-five of his original pieces, consisting of vaudevilles, opera librettos, romantic dramas, and comedies, were given more than a thousand performances. Today these works are largely forgotten, both in Denmark and abroad; but in Scandinavian theater history Andersen is significant for introducing many foreign styles, such as the French opéra comique and the Austrian folk play, into the Danish theater. Moreover, his experience with the theater influenced the way he shaped many of his stories and fairy tales, for it was through an appreciation of the stage that he developed his keen sense of observation and dramatic flare.

Frederick Marker states that Andersen "belonged among the younger exponents of romanticism but at the same time points ahead toward the realism which eventually triumphed in the 1870s. The production history of his plays provides a microcosm of the exotic, historical, idyllic, and topical elements that were the popular components of the colorful, romantic stage picture."[17]

Though it was through the theater that Andersen wished to claim ultimate recognition for his genius, the theater occasioned his most disastrous failures and the most bitter attacks against him. In turn, these caused him to react vociferously against the entire Danish nation, albeit in letters, journals, and private conversations, rarely in public.

Andersen's early notable plays were in the style of vaudeville, which he, along with Heiberg, helped make respectable in Denmark. Most of these light dramas feature plots about love and intrigue, often written in verse and incorporating well-known songs and music. Andersen tended to blend folk figures with situations typical of serious drama to poke fun at the foibles of high and low characters. His first production, *Love on St. Nicholas Tower*, parodied the romantic tragedy of the times by having a tailor and a watchman speak high verse and fight over the hand of a sweet maid of the lower classes. Though Andersen became less satirical in his vaudevilles over the years, most of his other successful plays, such as *The Invisible Man on Sprogø* (1839) and *The Bird in the Pear Tree* (1842), as well as his adaptations of Johann Nestroy's and Ferdinand Raimund's Austrian folk plays, follow the same pattern of parodying the social customs of Danes involved in a scandal or delicate love affair.

During the 1830s and 1840s Andersen also wrote librettos. His themes were often taken from romantic novels such as *The Festival at Kenilworth* (1836), based on a work by Sir Walter Scott. When he adapted his own dramatic poem *Agnete and the Merman* for the opera in 1843, it was a monumental flop, and the negative reaction by the public prompted a typically violent response by Andersen, who was in Paris at the time and wrote the following in his diary:

> At the Théâtre Palais-Royal in the evening and saw *Voyage between Heaven and Earth*. Schiern came and told me that the Berlingske News had said that Agnete had been hissed at. When I got home, I continued my letter to Jette Wulff: "May I never set eye on the home that only has eyes for my faults, but no heart for the great gifts that God has given me. I hate whatever hates me; I curse whatever curses me! — From Denmark are always coming the chill draughts that turn me to stone! They spit upon me; they trample me into the dirt! I have, though, a poetical nature, such as God hasn't given them many of! But which I will pray to Him the moment I die that He never give the nation more of! — Oh what venom is flowing through my veins during these hours! When I was young, I could cry; now I can't! I can only be proud, hate, despise, give my soul to the evil powers to find a moment's comfort! Here, in this big, strange city, Europe's most famous and noble personalities fondly surround me, meet with me as a kindred spirit; and at home boys sit spitting at my heart's dearest creation! Indeed, even if I am judged after my death, as I have been while I lived, I will have my day: the Danes are evil, cold, satanic — a people well-suited to the wet, moldy-green islands from where Tycho Brahe was exiled, where Leonora Ulfeldt was imprisoned, Ambrosius Stub was regarded as a jester by the nobility; and still many more will be ill treated like these, until this people's name will be legendary."[18] (29 April 1843)

The deep hurt and monumental conceit expressed here were reiterated time and again in Andersen's letters and journals. Andersen was unwilling to recognize that he was capable of writing poor works, and he expected to be flattered as he flattered others. Though he repeatedly asserted that he hated Denmark and the cultivated Danish society, he slavishly sought to shine in the eyes of his compatriots. Nor did he accept defeat. In 1846 he composed the libretto for I. P. E. Hartmann's *Liden Kirsten* (Little Christina, 1846), based on the true story of a princess who became a nun, and this "comeback" was a resounding success.

His most renowned play, however, was not an opera but a melodrama, *The Mulatto*, which showed the strong influence of French romantic drama, especially that of Victor Hugo. Based on the story *Les Épaves* ("The Waifs," 1838), by Fanny Reybaud, the drama concerns a young, sophisticated mulatto named Horatio, who writes poetry and runs his own plantation in Martinique. He rescues Cecille, the ward of a white plantation owner named La Rebellière, and La Rebellière's wife. Both women are captivated by Horatio's noble nature, and their esteem for the mulatto infuriates La Rebellière. So he contrives to have Horatio declared a slave and sold at auction. But Cecille comes of age at this point, declares her independence, and rescues Horatio by offering to marry him. The mulatto is thus vindicated in the eyes of society. As in the best of Andersen's plays and other works, this compelling social drama emphasizes his favorite fairy-tale themes, pariah, a neglected genius, shunned and persecuted by society, manages to overcome adversity and shine in the eyes of the world. This theme of emancipation appealed to the rising middle and lower classes in Denmark and reflected the dreams of glory shared by the people in this tiny nation. To this extent, Andersen often acted as the spokesman for a large majority of the people in Denmark, even though he was criticized for being inept.

The attacks on Andersen as a playwright ultimately drove him to assume a pseudonym in the 1840s. By producing his plays pseudonymously he hoped to avoid the vitriolic barbs of his critics. From 1845 until his death in 1875 he wrote for the Royal Theater and the Casino Theater, where vaudevilles were staged. It was during this period that he turned more toward fairy-tale dramas and comedies. For example, he wrote "*Lykkens Blomst*" (*The Blossom of Happiness*, 1845), which was about a forester who wishes to become a great person, such as a prince or a poet. This wish is granted by an elf, but the forester learns that the prince and the poet lead extremely difficult lives because of the responsibilities of their positions. As a result of this realization, he is overjoyed when given the chance to return to his former, humble occupation. Another play, *Meer end Perler og Guld* (*More than Pearls and Gold*, 1849), was an adaptation of *Raimund's Der Diamant des Geisterkönigs* (*The Diamond of the King of Spirits*, 1824). Here a young man is promised a statue of diamonds if he can find a young woman who has never lied. But once he finds her, he no longer wants to have the statue: she alone is worth more to him than all the riches in the world.

Andersen failed as a dramatist but, to his credit, he did stimulate many of his contemporaries to employ folk motifs, vernacular idioms, and fantasy in their plays. He may have had an influence even on Henrik Ibsen, whom he met. Whether this is the case or not, Andersen was clearly a forerunner in the Scandinavian movement that produced both Ibsen and August Strindberg. This can be seen in his adaptation of folk- and fairy-tale motifs for the theater. Throughout his life he occupied himself with the fantastic "other world" of the stage, but his plays never matched the artistry and luster of his fairy tales.

Nor did his novels, although he was at first recognized as one of Denmark's most promising novelists. When *The Improvisatore* appeared, it was an immediate success at home and highly praised thereafter in Germany and England. The impetus for the novel was Andersen's trip to Italy, where the action takes place. Antonio, a poor orphan with an amazingly poetic nature, has the good fortune to come under the patronage of a rich patrician family in Rome. He is sent to a Jesuit school, where he excels as a student and makes the acquaintance of the handsome and wild Bernardo, who leaves the school to become an officer. In the meantime, despite the severe discipline of the school and the criticism of his benefactors, Antonio develops his artistic skill as an improvisator. After a reunion with Bernardo, he makes the acquaintance of Annunziata, a great Spanish-Italian singer. Both Bernardo and Antonio fall in love with her, and naturally they fight a duel over the beautiful young woman. After the first shot Antonio thinks mistakenly that he has killed his friend. He flees to the south of Italy, joins a band of robbers, leaves the robbers, and continues to have many adventures until he establishes a name for himself as an improvisator in the theater. Eventually he learns that Bernardo is alive, and he can return to the patrician society of Rome as a success. Indeed, he even marries an ethereal young woman named Maria, whom he had once believed to be blind.

This autobiographical romance is based on the structure of the German *Künstlerroman*, in which a young man rebels against society to develop his skills independently as an artist. The artist remains a rebel, and often he makes his way to a type of paradise, representing freedom of the imagination, or dies in the attempt. This is the pattern in Tieck's *Franz Sternbalds Wanderungen* (*Franz Sternbald's Wanderings*, 1798), Novalis's *Heinrich von Ofterdingen* (1802), and Hoffmann's *Der goldene Topf* (*The Golden Pot*, 1814). Andersen broke with the general romantic pattern somewhat by having his artist return to the fold of society, where he obliges his bene-factors to recognize his particular greatness as an artist. In this regard, his novel also reflects the influence of the German *Bildungsroman* (novel of development, especially Goethe's *Wilhelm Meisters Lehrjahre* [*Wilhelm Meister's Apprentice Years*], 1795–96), in which the protagonist eventually abandons the theater to assume a responsible position in society.

Obviously, Andersen's work was a thinly veiled depiction of his own life and problems, and he preferred to champion the artist rather than established social leaders. In fact, he had once been criticized by Heiberg for being too much of a lyrical improvisator, and there is no doubt but that Andersen was bent on responding to Heiberg by showing the posi-tive aspects of versatility and improvisation. Though he impressed his contemporary readers by blending romance and adventure with surrealis-tic descriptions of the Italian landscape, the melodrama and bombastic language make the book difficult if not painful to read today. Like all his longer prose narratives, the novel is pretentious and derivative. By en-deavoring to resemble the great German novelists he admired, Andersen became nothing but their pale shadow.

However, he did have success in his own day, and this success moved him to write other romances. He followed *The Improvisatore* with *O. T.* (1836) and *Only a Fiddler* (1837), both set in Denmark. Again he mixed obvious autobiographical elements with fictional projections to illustrate his philosophy of genius. Andersen was intrigued by the character of the moody Byronic hero and thought of himself in these terms. In *O. T.*, his protagonist, Otto Thostrup, a brooding, mysterious character, has his initials tattooed on his shoulder. They stand for his name and for the Odense jail, in which his mother had been imprisoned. Otto and a twin sister were born in the Odense jail. When his mother dies, he is adopted by a rich baron while his unknown sister is left to drift among the dregs of society. Haunted by this past, Otto seeks to clear his mother's name and find his sister. All this is accomplished with the help of his close friend Wilhelm. In the end Otto is no longer sullen and strange, and he looks forward to marriage with one of Wilhelm's sisters.

In *Only a Fiddler* the ending is not so happy. Here Andersen depicts the tragicomic lives of a poor boy named Christian and a rich Jewish girl named Naomi. They are drawn to each other as children but are separated by events. Naomi is raised in Copenhagen, becomes spoiled, snubs Christian, runs away with a Polish riding master, and eventually marries a French count, with whom she is unhappy. Christian does not lead such an adventurous life. Though a gifted musician, he plods along, never receiving the help he needs to realize his genius. He dies as a village musician in humble circumstances.

In both novels Andersen portrays the mores and manners of Danish society and shows how young men of genius from the lower classes must overcome obstacles to gain recognition. Though Christian never realizes his genius, it is clear that he is gifted, and that if he were helped in the right way by the upper classes he might achieve greatness and happiness. Otto's case in *O. T.* is different because influential people aid him, and success is guaranteed.

The social mobility and immobility of talented people intrigued Andersen, and he turned to this theme again in *De to Baronesser* (*The Two Baronesses*, 1848). This novel, filled with one incredible event after another, demonstrates that honest Hermann, the grandson of an eccentric old baroness who has worked her way up from the lower classes, deserves to marry a poor girl who has braved misfortune to keep her virtue. Both young people display the diligence necessary for success; theirs is a marriage of noble minds.

In later years Andersen attempted to write a philosophical novel about genius triumphing over agnosticism and despair. In *To Be or Not to Be?* (1857) Niels Bryde, the moody protagonist, succumbs to the temptation of evolutionary and materialist theories based on the ideas of the German philosophers David Friedrich Strauss and Ludwig Feuerbach. He loses his Christian faith, only to recover it when he realizes there is an immortality of the soul that manifests itself in every particle of life.

In *Lucky Peter* (1870), Andersen's last novel, he returns to the structure of the *Künstlerroman* to reflect on his own life and genius. Again we have the rise to fame of the chosen son of common people. Peter, the poor but talented son of a coachman, is born in the same house as Felix, a rich merchant's son, and their lives are contrasted. Felix amounts to nothing more than a mediocre but rich merchant; Peter achieves greatness because he pursues his destiny with unerring zeal. When he is only a boy, his musical talent is recognized, and he is given schooling that enables him to enjoy a meteoric career. Eventually he writes an opera appropriately entitled *Aladdin*, and after receiving a thunderous ovation for singing the title role at the premiere, he collapses and dies. This melodramatic novel appears to be based on Wilhelm Wackenroder's story "Der Tonkünstler Joseph Berglinger" (*The Musical Artist Joseph Berglinger*," 1796), in which the hero dies at the greatest moment of his career. Andersen tries to enhance this familiar success story with colorful portraits of Danish social life, but the novel suffers from a contrived plot and didactic commentary. The more he repeats the same plot and ideas, the more trite and unconvincing they become.

Andersen was never able to master long narrative prose. He was overly conscious of his models in Tieck, Jean Paul, Goethe, Hoffmann, and Scott, and his novels lack their humor, subtlety of thought, self-reflection, philosophical depth, and variety of theme. At times there are remarkable passages in his novels, especially passages describing country life and customs, but they are generally undercut by an insistent moralistic tone. Only when he forgets that he must follow a prescribed form to justify his life and ideas or to match the work of a famous novelist is he capable of introducing extraordinary chapters that come alive through closeness of observation and penetrating insights.

Andersen's poetry and travel books are similarly uneven. His initial book of poetry, *Digte*, was followed quickly by *Phantasier og Skizzer* (*Fantasies and Sketches*) in 1831. The first contains humorous poems for the most part; the second, melancholy love poems and occasional verse. Andersen could write all types of poetry with great facility. He composed most of his plays and librettos in verse and continued to publish volumes of poetry throughout his life, but he failed to break new ground as a poet because of his derivative styles. His best poems by far are the personal love lyrics; these are deeply felt expressions of longing and despair. In his other lyrical endeavors, he covers a broad range of topics, from folklore and national history to subjects pertaining to children. Though he always satisfies formal requirements of meter and rhythm, he brings nothing new to the themes and forms he employs.

Andersen was at his best when he could experiment with personal experience in his own idiom. This is evident in his first travel book, *Journey on Foot from Holmens Canal to the East Point of Amager*, a humorous and fantastic depiction of a journey, similar to Hoffmann's series of stories titled "Kreisleriana in Fantasiestücke" in *Callots Manier* (1814–15). Andersen weaves together dream elements, literary references to Tieck, Jean Paul, A. W. Iffland, August Kotzebue, Chamisso, and Goethe, and vivid depictions of landscape to create an intoxicating effect. In his other travel books, such as *A Poet's Bazaar* (1842), *In Sweden* (1851), *In Spain* (1863), and *A Visit to Portugal* (1868), Andersen mixes impressions, anecdotes, observations, stories, and literary topics with descriptions of the countries and peoples he visited. In addition, he includes comments on the changing times. As he was perhaps the most widely traveled author in the nineteenth century, Andersen's notes on customs, portraits of prominent people, and depictions of his own experiences were illuminating for readers of his own time and are still fascinating today. In particular, *In Sweden* contains a highly significant chapter entitled "Poetry's California," in which he argues that literature must keep pace with modern technological developments. If the future belongs to the sciences, then literature must adjust and reflect the new inventions in order to point out the miraculous aspects of life:

> The sunlight of science must penetrate the poet; he must perceive truth and harmony in the minute and in the immensely great with a clear eye: it must purify and enrich the understanding and imagination, and show him new forms that will supply to him more animated words. Even single discoveries will furnish a new flight. What fairy tales cannot the world unfold under the microscope.... Science always unfolds something new; light and truth are everything that is created — beam out from hence with eternally divine clearness. Mighty image of God, do thou illumine and enlighten mankind; and when its intellectual eye is accustomed to the luster, the new Aladdin will come, and thou, man, shalt with him, who concisely clear, and richly sings the beauty of truth wander through Poetry's California.[19]

Andersen thought of himself as a poetic harbinger of truth and wisdom, a prophet whose versatility should be acclaimed if not glorified as the new Aladdin. He sought to stamp his times with his plays, novels, and travel books, and to a certain extent he succeeded in Denmark during the nineteenth century. But he made his lasting international contribution to art in a form in which he least expected to achieve immortality.

The Tales

Although Andersen knew he was a simple "tailor" of humble origin, he preferred to depict himself as a "romantic" fairy-tale hero, a misunderstood genius or glorified Aladdin. He suspected, however, that audiences and critics saw him differently and might even despise him. The more he tried to dismiss his suspicions and fears, the more he was troubled by nervous disorders and psychic disturbances. To contend with his self-doubts and perhaps to rationalize his behavior, he made use of Ørsted's ideas in *The Soul in Nature* (1850) and combined them with his own animistic belief in Christianity. Andersen met Ørsted while he was a student in Slagelse, and the older man had a great influence on him throughout his life. He became an early mentor as well as substitute father for Andersen, who was very receptive to his ideas. Ørsted argued that the laws of nature are the thoughts of God, and, as the spirit of nature becomes projected, reality assumes the form of miracle that only a few talented people can reveal. At one point in *The Soul in Nature*, Ørsted asserts:

> All the distinct and simple truths in man, as we have seen, are revelations of Eternal Reason. He therefore who discovers and declares them, is so far an instrument in the hands of God. In as much as the revealed truth is higher, more comprehensive, and more exalting, it is proportionally supernatural in comparison with that finite condition which at a lower estimate is exclusively called Nature, although it is perfectly natural in the eternal nature of God. One external sign of the exalted nature of this revelation is the vastness of its operation; vast, let it be observed, not merely by its great extension through the world, but in the amount of the effect which it produces in the human race itself — the improvement, the exaltation, the nearer approach to God, of which mankind thus becomes conscious.[20]

Such views were readily accepted and adopted by Andersen, who felt that he was "an instrument of God." If life was divinely miraculous, then God also protected his "elect" and provided help when they needed it. Power is located in the hands of God, and only before Him does one have to bow. We shall see how he worked out these ideas in his tales. In truth, however, Andersen submitted more to a temporal, social system based on aristocratic-bourgeois hegemony than to God, and he had to rationalize the social relations of domination so that he could live with himself. As we know, he tried to deny his class origins and repress his rebellious feelings in order to gain money, comfort, praise, and freedom to exercise his occupation as writer. And as an aspiring *Digter*, he endeavored both to imitate great poets and to find his own voice and style to depict the social contradictions he had difficulty resolving for himself. Such a situation meant a life of self-doubt and anxiety.

It was not, therefore, from joy and exuberance that Andersen wrote his fairy tales; it was more from a sense of profound suffering, disappointment, chagrin, and resentment, if not rage. Obviously he also derived great pleasure in composing these stories, and he retained a naive appreciation of his immediate surroundings and experiences that served to inspire his writing. Yet he was fundamentally driven to write most of his tales to quell the anguish he felt as he made his daily compromises to become a great Digter.

Altogether he wrote 156 tales. The first collection, *Eventyr fortalte for Børn* (*Fairy Tales Told for Children*, 1835), consisted of "The Tinder Box," "The Princess on the Pea," "Little Claus and Big Claus," and "Little Ida's Flowers." With the exception of "Little Ida's Flowers," these stories were adaptations of folk tales expressly designed for a young audience, but in reality, since Andersen had little experience with children and children's literature, they were tales that appealed to and were intended to appeal to adults. That same year, in the second printing of the tales, he added "Thumbelina," "The Naughty Boy," and "The Traveling Companion." In 1837, as the collection grew more successful, he provided two more tales, "The Little Mermaid" and "The Emperor's New Clothes," and in each subsequent edition until 1843 he dedicated the tales to children. Thereafter, the title of his fairy-tale anthologies was changed to *Nye Eventyr* (*New Fairy Tales*), a more accurate indication of the direction Andersen was taking: he no longer wrote "exclusively" for young audiences (if he ever had), and many of his compositions even broke away from the fairy-tale genre.

Andersen wrote fables, allegories, anecdotes, legends, satires, farces, philosophical commentaries, and didactic stories. In general he developed and revitalized the German genre of the *Kunstmärchen*, or literary as opposed to oral tales, which had become popular in Europe by the beginning of the nineteenth century. Such gifted writers as Ludwig Tieck, Wilhelm Heinrich Wackenroder, Novalis, Clemens Brentano, Achim von Arnim, Joseph von Eichendorff, Friedrich de La Motte-Fouqué, Adalbert Chamisso, E. T. A. Hoffmann, and Wilhelm Hauff had reworked folklore and introduced fantastic events and characters, together with complex ideas and subtle styles, into their tales. Their compositions were conceived to meet the tastes and needs of a middle-class reading public, whereas the oral folk tales catered to the taste of the lower classes and peasantry. Stimulated by the German romantics, Andersen gradually developed his own peculiar themes, a refreshing, humorous style, and lively colloquial dialogue. Many critics in his day frowned on his idiosyncratic use of Danish as vulgar, but it was just this unconventional colloquial quality that made his appeal unique. Moreover, like the German romantics, Andersen demonstrated how fantastic literature could be devastatingly realistic in its symbolic allusion to social contradictions.

In his autobiography, *Das Märchen meines Lebens ohne Dichtung*, Andersen remarks that:

> the fairy tales became reading matter for children and adults.… They found open doors and open hearts in Denmark. Everyone read them. Then I eliminated the phrase "told for children" and followed this with three books of "new tales," which I created myself, and which were highly praised. I could not have wished for anything better. I felt anxious, afraid that I could not justify so much honor in my time. My heart was invigorated by the rays of sunshine. I gained courage and was greatly motivated to develop myself more in this direction and to pay more attention to the rich source from which I had to create. There is definitely progress to be found when one follows the order in which I wrote my fairy tales. One can notice my ideas taking clearer shape, a greater restraint in the use of my medium, and, if I may say, more healthy qualities and a natural freshness.[21]

It is difficult to know exactly what the "healthy qualities" in his tales are. If for Andersen "healthy" meant greater control over disquieting feelings, masterly sublimation, greater adaptation to frustrating conditions, and artful self-deception, then the tales do reflect "healthy qualities." Yet these same qualities conceal often-overlooked "unhealthy" ideas about social conditions and personal problems that were woven into his narratives. These were dangerous ideas that stemmed from Andersen's own feelings of oppression and troubled his conscience. Too many readers regard Andersen's works ahistorically and universalize the symbolic formations of his tales as though the author and his social context were insignificant. They lose sight of the artist, his struggles, and his contribution to the evolution of the fairy-tale genre. In Andersen's case, a critical, historical approach to his tales raises some interesting questions about their contradictory features and their reception in English-speaking countries.

Elias Bredsdorff has noted that only 30 of Andersen's 156 tales[22] have been reprinted in many different translations, some accurate, many not. The tales that have been printed and circulated most in the United States and the United Kingdom are: "The Tinder Box," "Little Claus and Big Claus," "The Princess on the Pea," "Little Ida's Flowers," "Thumbelina," and "The Traveling Companion" (1835); "The Little Mermaid" and "The Emperor's New Clothes" (1837); "The Steadfast Tin Soldier" and "The Wild Swans" (1838); "The Garden of Eden," "The Flying Trunk," and "The Storks" (1839); "Willie Winkie," "The Swineherd," and "The Buckwheat" (1841); "The Nightingale," "The Top and the Ball," and "The Ugly Duckling" (1843); "The Fir Tree" and "The Snow Queen"(1844); "The Darning Needle," "The Elf Hill," "The Red Shoes," "The Shepherdess and the Chimney Sweep," and "The Little Match Girl" (1845); "The Shadow" (1847); and "The Old House," "The Happy Family," and "The Shirt Collar" (1848). Given the fact that these are the "classic" Andersen tales in English, it is worth commenting on their general features before evaluating other tales.

Although Andersen's stories have suffered from the clumsy hands of censors and poor translators up through the 1940s, two fairly reliable editions of his complete short prose narratives have made his entire canon accessible to the English-reading public: one translated by Jean Hersholt, the other by Erik Christian Haugaard. A smaller but very good selection of translated tales can be found in Patricia Conroy and Sven Rossel's *Tales and Stories by Hans Christian Andersen* (1980). More recently, Diana Crone Frank, Jeffrey Frank, and Tiina Nunnally have produced new excellent translations in 2003 and 2004.[23] Despite these fine works, it must be admitted that the full flavor of Andersen's unusual use of the Danish language is difficult to capture. Folk rhythms and colloquialisms, childlike humor and startling puns, topical and historical references, local color and cultural associations — all these have given him a special reception in Denmark, where he is considered distinctively Danish, the spokesman of the common people, the representative of a vigorous nineteenth-century cultural force. But he is also one of the key figures in the development of the literary fairy tale in the world at large, primarily as the genre has been cultivated for children in the West.[24]

Andersen's tales were among the first considered suitable and proper enough for the nurseries and households of respectable nineteenth-century middle-class families. It must be remembered that in both the United Kingdom and the United States, the fairy tale had been stamped as subversive and suspect from the eighteenth century to the middle of the nineteenth century. It was not regarded as moral and instructive enough for the emerging bourgeois sensibility, which stressed utilitarian values, obedience, sexual abstinence, and Christian virtues. This is not to say that fairy tales for children were banned. Rather, there was a limited market for them, since most educators, religious writers, and publishers waged a war against the pagan, superstitious, and irrational features of folk and fairy tales. Certainly, the magical tales thrived in the oral tradition and had been spread by word of mouth for centuries. But they had not yet been fully approved and refined for the upper classes in print form. Only toward the end of the eighteenth century did it appear that they might provide amusement and pleasure for children. All the more reason that religious leaders and educators continued to voice their opinion against these allegedly common and immoral tales, and such a campaign made middle-class families wary of purchasing the tales. At the beginning of the nineteenth century, however, there was a successful countercampaign in England and America, and by the 1820s translations of the tales collected by the Brothers Grimm appeared and helped make the fairy tale "respectable." Other books by German and British romantics that defended imaginative works and fairy tales soon appeared, and later such major Victorian writers as John Ruskin, Charles Dickens, William Makepeace Thackeray, George MacDonald, and Lewis Carroll wrote fantastic tales for children and spoke out in defense of this imaginative literature. Moreover, fairy tales had always been popular in their chapbook or cheapbook form, small booklets published during the eighteenth and early nineteenth centuries that circulated on the Continent and in England.

It was exactly at the point that the fairy tale was becoming more and more popular among middle-class readers that Andersen himself, influenced by the German romantics, Dickens, and the Danish romantic movement, began to insert himself into the debate. His participation in the literary discourse on fairy tales was not a deliberate critical act, but rather the outcome of his naive interest and predilection. Andersen had always been captivated by fairy tales as stories and dramas, and in 1834–35 he began to concoct a recipe for the fairy tales that were to bear his imprint: he rewrote folk tales, added a dose of Christian moralism mixed with bourgeois individualism, stirred the ingredients with folk humor, and ladled everything out in a vernacular style. The more comfortable he felt with adapting the folk tradition, the more he began to invent his own imaginative tales. His aim was to please and, at times, to provoke children and adults of all classes.

If we look at those tales that made Andersen famous in England and America (and are still the most popular), it is striking that they are the ones written primarily from 1835 to 1848, the tales Andersen composed allegedly for children that were just as successful with adults. These thirty tales are serious and colorful variations on a few personal themes. The major ideas concern the recognition of artistic genius, nobility of mind versus nobility of blood, the exposure of class injustice and hypocrisy, the master-servant relationship, the immortality of the soul, and the omnipotence and omnipresence of God. Almost all the tales touched on Andersen's private desires and functioned psychologically to provide him with secret revenge or to justify his dubious actions to himself. The focus in my limited discussion will be on the hidden, ambivalent features of "The Tinder Box," "The Princess on the Pea," "The Emperor's New Clothes," "The Nightingale," "The Ugly Duckling," and "The Red Shoes," but I shall also examine some other key tales in his oeuvre.

"The Tinder Box" reveals how closely Andersen at first adhered to the patterns of the folk-tale tradition when he began writing fairy tales.[25] Characteristic of a number of the magic folk tales (*Zaubermärchen*) is the rise of an adventurous hero who depends on his own talents and gifts from strangers to attain wealth and happiness. Generally speaking, the pro-tagonist is downtrodden, oppressed, the youngest member of a family, or a small person; but he is always clever and knows how to make use of his abilities. Once the protagonist is assigned a task or cast into the world, he usually has three encounters with gift-bearing creatures (giants, dwarfs, animals, fairies), and it appears that he will triumph easily. At the peak of his first rise in fortunes, however, there is a sudden fall, or peripeteia, and the hero must call on friends and his own resources to renew his rise to power and riches. As oral stories, the magic folk tales were transcribed in simple, blunt language by Jacob and Wilhelm Grimm and other collec-tors such as the Danish storyteller Mathias Winther[26] at the beginning of the nineteenth century. Description and characterization were kept to a minimum. The paratactic sentences were built up with careful transitions so that clearly defined binary oppositions of good and evil could be im-mediately observed. From the outset the reader or listener of a folk tale knows that the narrative perspective is partial to the hero, who is bound to succeed; the question is always how. The magic of the oral tale, while important, depends not so much on its miraculous quality in the tale it-self as on the ingenuity of the narrator in using the arsenal of folk motifs to vary well- known schemes so that they will touch on the dreams and needs of the audience.

The *Tinderbox* (1887) illustrated by Jospeh J. Mora in *Hans Andersen's Fairy Tales*

In writing "The Tinderbox," Andersen employs the folk motif of the disgruntled soldier who, after years of loyal service, is discharged without due compensation by an ungrateful king. This lowly soldier seeks revenge and wins the hand of a princess. This tale type can also be found in several of the Grimms' tales, such as "The Blue Light," "How Six Made

Their Way in the World," and "Brother Lustig."[27] Andersen transforms this plot into a tale that mirrored the wishes of many maltreated, smart young men of the lower and middle classes. The rags-to-riches theme is central to his witty narrative about a young soldier, who by chance meets a disgusting witch whose lower lip hangs all the way down to her chest. He agrees to help her haul money and a tinderbox from a hole in the ground but then chops off her head when she will not tell him why she wants the tinderbox. He goes to town, takes quarters at an inn, lives sumptuously and merrily. He attends the theater, goes for drives in the king's park, and gives money to the poor because he remembers what it felt like not to have a penny in his pocket. When his "luck" runs out, however, he falls as quickly as he had risen in social esteem, and his fair-weather friends abandon him. A type of Aladdin figure, he accidentally discovers the magic of the tinderbox and the power of the three dogs that can provide him with anything he needs. Here Andersen subconsciously concocts a sociopolitical formula that was the keystone of bourgeois progress and success in the nineteenth century: use talents to acquire money and perhaps a wife, establish a system of continual recapitalization (tinderbox and three dogs) to guarantee income and power, and employ money and power to maintain social and political hegemony. The soldier is justified in his use of power and money because he is essentially better than anyone else — chosen to rule. The king and queen are dethroned, and the soldier rises to assume control of society through the application of his innate talents and good fortune.

The ironic tone of Andersen's writing, the melodious rhythms, the terse, delightful descriptions, and the dramatic sequences transform an oral folk tale into a colorful literary fairy tale that glimmers with hope. Instead of "once upon a time," Andersen begins the narrative on an unusual note: "A soldier came marching down the road:... right! Left ... right! He had a pack on his back and a sword at his side. He had been in the war and he was on his way home."[28] The witch admires his sword and knapsack and, convinced that he is a real soldier, willingly gives him all the money he wants. On a psychological level, the killing of the witch followed by the dethronement of the king and queen and the soldier's triumph as "true prince" are the sublimated artistic means Andersen uses to gain revenge on his mother, benefactors, and critics. All this is done with humor throughout the narrative, and there is a delightful picture of Andersen's wish fulfillment at the end of the tale once the king and queen are sent flying into the air (p. 7):

The royal guards got frightened; and the people began to shout: "Little soldier, you shall be our king and marry the princess."

The soldier rode in the king's golden carriage; and the three dogs danced in front of it and barked: "Hurrah!"

The little boys whistled and the royal guards presented arms. The princess came out of her copper castle and became queen, which she liked very much. The wedding feast lasted a week; and the three dogs sat at the table and made eyes at everyone.

Andersen must have derived immense personal satisfaction in writing this "radical" tale of role reversals, for underneath the humor is dead seriousness, an urge to express his social hostility and to prove himself at all costs. On another level, the tale can be read by children (and adults, of course) as a tale of the sexual and social maturation of a young person in a "dog-eat-dog" world. The soldier has a knapsack (mind, talents) and sword (power, phallus), and in confrontation with the outer world he learns not to waste his sexual and mental powers but to control and direct them to gain happiness. The psychological impulse of the tale is connected to Andersen's obvious criticism of the hypocrisy and injustice of the aristocracy. Throughout the tale, he depicts their artificiality, which is supplanted by the "true nobility" of his young, lower-class soldier.

"The Princess on the Pea" is also a tale about "true nobility," but told with tongue in cheek. A princess proves to be genuine when she feels a pea placed under twenty mattresses. This pea is then exhibited in the royal museum after her happy marriage with the prince, who had been seeking an authentic princess. Obviously Andersen was poking fun at the curious and ridiculous measures taken by the nobility to establish the value of bloodlines. On the other hand, he makes an argument for sensitivity as the decisive factor in determining the authenticity of royalty. Andersen never tired of glorifying the sensitive nature of an elite class of people. This sensitivity is spelled out in different ways in other tales of 1835, such as "Little Ida's Flowers," "Thumbelina," and "The Traveling Companion." In all these stories, "small" or oppressed people cultivate their special talents and struggle to realize their goals despite the forces of adversity. Ida retains and fulfills her dreams of flowers by resisting a crass professor's vicious attacks. Thumbelina survives many hazardous adventures to marry the king of the angels. Johannes, a poor orphan, promises to be good so that God will protect him, and indeed his charitable deeds lead to a marriage with a princess. All the gifted but disadvantaged characters, who are God-fearing, come into their own in Andersen's tales. In contrast, the rich and privileged are either ridiculed or exposed as insensitive, cruel, and unjust.

Perhaps the most amusing and famous of Andersen's tales about "false nobility," a story that has been adapted for film, television, and the radio many times, is "The Emperor's New Clothes." Here an emperor is literally robbed and denuded in front of our eyes because he has wasted his time and money on beautiful new clothes instead of carrying out his responsibilities. Andersen quickly sets the tone of the narrative by taking his readers into his confidence and relating how two swindlers plan to trick the emperor and the parasites at court. We laugh at the foolish emperor as the plot develops, and then Andersen aptly introduces the courageous small child who cries: "But he doesn't have anything on!" (p. 81). By having a child speak the truth, Andersen emphasizes a learning process that relies on common sense and a perception of the contradictions in society. Seeing is depicted in this tale as the courage of one's convictions, and this depiction may be a major reason for the narrative's appeal for young readers, who are too often told "to see with your eyes and not with your mouth." For Andersen, sight must become insight, which in turn demands action.

Yet Andersen cannot be considered an antiauthoritarian writer, a champion of emancipatory children's literature. The courageous acts of his heroes are often undercut by their self-denial, humility, and willingness to sacrifice themselves in the service of a benevolent king or God. One of the classic examples of this type of tale is "The Little Mermaid," which harks back to the folk stories of a water urchin desirous of obtaining a soul so she can marry the human being she loves. Andersen also knew Fouqué's *Undine* (1811) and Goethe's "Die Neue Melusine" ("The New Melusine," 1812), stories about the aspirations of pagan water sprites. However, his tale about the self-sacrificing mermaid is distinctly different from the narratives by Goethe and Fouqué, who, perhaps out of their own sense of guilt for the tendency of upper-class men to seduce and abandon lower-class women, punished their noblemen for forgetting their Christian values and manners. Andersen's perspective focuses on the torture and suffering that a member of the "lower species" must undergo to gain a soul. Characteristically, he allows the mermaid to rise out of the water and move in the air of royal circles only after her tongue is removed and her tail transformed into legs, described as "sword-like" when she walks or dances. Voiceless and tortured, the mermaid serves a prince who never fully appreciates her worth. Twice she saves his life.

The second time is most significant: instead of killing him to regain her identity and rejoin her sisters and grandmother, the mermaid forfeits her own life and becomes an ethereal figure blessed by God. If she does good deeds for the next three hundred years, she will be endowed with an immortal soul. Her divine mission consists of flying through the homes of human beings as an invisible spirit. If she finds a good child, who makes his parents happy and deserves their love, her sentence will be shortened. A naughty and mean child can lengthen the three hundred years she must serve in God's name.

But the question remains whether or not the mermaid is really acting in God's name. Her falling in love with royalty and all her subsequent actions involve self-denial and rationalization. The mermaid's sense of herself becomes divided and diminished because she is attracted to a class of people who will never accept her on her own terms. To join her supposed superiors she must practically slit her own throat, and though she realizes that she can never truthfully express who she is and what she wants, she is unwilling to return to her own species. Thus she must somehow justify her existence to herself through abstinence and self-abnegation — a behavior preached by the bourgeoisie of the time, but certainly not characteristically practiced by the nobility and upper classes.

Paradoxically, Andersen seems to be arguing that true virtue and self-realization can be obtained through self-denial. The artistic conception of this paradox emanated from his own experience as a gangly, lower-class youngster who sought to cultivate himself through constant compromise and subjugation to external laws. By becoming voiceless, walking with legs like swords, and denying one's own needs, one will allegedly gain divine recognition for one's essential genius, a metaphor for the educated nod of approval from the dominant class. The absence of the nod underscores the fact that the dominant class only gives its approval to those from "below the surface" who are prepared to perform sacrificial acts in an effort to rise above their "natural" station in life. Nobility is indeed of the mind, but it also needs connections with nobility of the blood to succeed in the real world.

Andersen consistently defended notions of self-abandonment and self-deprivation in the name of aristocratic-bourgeois laws and standards designed to make members of the lower classes into tractable, obedient citizens. Such conformist thinking stemmed from the obsequious "tailor" side of his personality. As eager as he was for his genius to shine, he was just as eager to please, and just as ready to humiliate himself before

The Nightingale (1900) Illustrated by W. Heath Robinson in *Hans Andersen's Fairy Tales*

wealthy, powerful patrons. He could never forget the poverty that he suffered in his hometown of Odense that made him feel inferior and want to transcend it. Sometimes he associated it with a swamp. At other times he transformed Odense into an idyllic town, and he clearly enjoyed reading his stories aloud to Copenhagen blue-collar workers as he also sought out the company of common people during his journeys abroad. He was never certain as to whether he should be proud of his common background or ashamed. Both "The Nightingale" and "The Ugly Duckling," two of Andersen's most finely wrought tales, reveal how he sought to master his dilemma by turning it into a type of success story.

On the surface, "The Nightingale," which I discuss more thoroughly in the following chapter, appears to record the triumph of a common artist, portrayed as the nightingale, who has enormous talent. Indeed, the Chinese emperor almost dies because he abandons the common nightingale with the beautiful voice. Only the bird's art can save him. However, it is also clear in this complex story that the bird wants and seeks the connection to royalty. In brief, after the nightingale is humbled, he returns to the emperor, for it is clear that in a system of patronage, even a gifted artist cannot live without serving the aristocracy.

This is also the implied message of "The Ugly Duckling," in which Andersen again uses a fowl to represent an ordinary person who is extraordinary. In this well-known story a little swan, who is made to think he is an ugly duckling, discovers his true identity as a beautiful member of an aristocratic class of birds. The tale is pure wish fulfillment and celebrates the rise of a humble person to great heights, but Andersen also conveys his secret disdain for the masses and his longing to be accepted by court society. The young swan does not return "home" but lands in a beautiful garden where he is admired by children and adults. Beauty for the swan is measured by the "royal" swans and by the well-behaved children and people in the garden. In the end, the swan's growth and flight become an apology for Andersen's elitist thinking.

Still, the tale has positive psychological features. As a fairy tale for children, the narrative suggests that each child has the potential to liberate himself or herself from oedipal ties, to overcome social obstacles, and to gain recognition — Andersen's greatest wish fulfillment. The transformation of the ugly duckling into a beautiful swan can thus be interpreted as the confirmation of dreams experienced by numerous children, regardless of class. It can also be considered as a revelation of the duckling's true inner being that reinforced Andersen's essentialist thinking. Yet the swan, like the nightingale, becomes a tame bird. Andersen, who loved to wander about Europe like a bird and then return home to bask in the praise of royalty and upper-class friends, constantly used this metaphor for himself.[29] It is also interesting that, unlike most folk tales in which the hero becomes independent and omnipotent, Andersen's birdlike geniuses soar high only to return to earth.

Although docile and kind on the surface, Andersen was often merciless in his tales, especially when it came to curbing the pride of rebellious figures who need to be taught a lesson. In "The Red Shoes," Karen, a poor orphan, mistakenly believes that a generous old woman adopted her because she wears red shoes (a symbol of vanity, sexuality, and sin). Although Karen tries to abandon the shoes, she cannot resist their allure. Interestingly, this story, like "The Ugly Duckling," is about misrecognition. The little swan is misrecognized and cannot recognize himself until he is in his proper milieu. Karen feels she is better than she is and does not recognize who she is until she, too, is placed in her proper milieu. So she must be taken to task by a stern angel, who sentences her to dance without stopping.

The only way Karen can end the angel's sentence is by requesting the municipal executioner to cut off her feet. Once this is done, she is recognized for the charitable work that she does while she lives in the house of the local minister. Upon her death, Karen's soul "flew on a sun-beam up to God" (p. 294). This ghastly tale — reminiscent of the gory, pedagogical bestseller of Andersen's time and later, the German Heinrich Hoffmann's *Struwwelpeter* (1845) — is a detailed description of the punishment that awaits young children who dare to oppose authority, and I shall also deal with this tale and Andersen's concern with children more thoroughly in Chapter three. Here I just want to note how Andersen repeatedly stressed that acceptance into God's kingdom depends on obedience, service, and self-restraint. In actuality he spoke not for God but for the standards of discipline and punishment instituted in Danish society. Pedagogically, the themes of Andersen's fairy tales for children comply with the norms and values of traditional Christian education. Needless to say, his classical status today is based on his acceptance of norms that still prevail in the realms of children's literature.

Yet Andersen's fame in English-speaking countries does not rest solely on his fairy tales directed at children. Such an intriguing, subtle story as "The Shadow" reveals Andersen as a significant precursor of surrealist and existentialist literature. As many critics have noted, this haunting narrative is highly autobiographical; it stems from the humiliation Andersen suffered when Edvard Collin adamantly rejected his proposal to use the familiar "you" (du) in their discourse — and there was more than one such rejection. By retaining the formal "you" (de), Collin undoubtedly asserting his class superiority, and this was meant to remind Andersen of the social distance that separated them. Though they had come to regard each other as brothers during their youth, Collin held firmly to propriety. He controlled a certain portion of Andersen's life — something that the writer actually desired, but also resented — and he wanted to keep a certain distance from Andersen to prevent his personal relationship with him from deteriorating into what he considered disorderly intimacy occasioned by Andersen's impositions.

In "The Shadow," Andersen clearly sought to avenge himself through his tale about a philosopher's shadow that separates itself from its owner and becomes immensely rich and successful. When it becomes a person in its own right and returns to visit the scholar,[30] the shadow/Andersen puts the philosopher/Collin in his place by refusing to use the familiar du, and then he explains that it was poetry that made a human being out of him. Not only does the shadow become humanlike, but he gains power over other people through his ability to see evil. Ironically, the shadow's sinister talents allow him to improve his fortunes, whereas the philosopher, who can only write about the beautiful and the good, becomes poor and neglected. Eventually the philosopher is obliged to travel with his former shadow — the shadow now as master, and the master as shadow. When the shadow deceives a princess to win her hand in marriage, the philosopher threatens to reveal the truth about him. The crafty shadow, however, convinces the princess that the philosopher himself is a deranged shadow, and she decides to have him killed to end his misery.

The reversal of fortunes and power relations is not a process of liberation but one of revenge. Andersen's wish fulfillment was directed not only at Collin but at all his superiors, whether they were benefactors or enemies. Yet to see "The Shadow" merely as the product of a personal grudge is to do it an injustice. Andersen ingeniously reworks the folk motif of Chamisso's *Peter Schlemihls wundersame Geschichte* (1814), in which a young man sells his shadow to the devil to become rich; and he also explores the Hegelian notion of master-servant in a fascinating way. The shadow-servant, who is closer to the material conditions of life than the intellectual owner of his services, is able to take advantage of what he sees and experiences — the basic conditions of social life — to overthrow his master; whereas the master, who has been able to experience reality only through the mediation of his shadow, is too idealistic to defend himself. From a philosophical viewpoint Andersen questions the idea of autonomous identity; from a psychological viewpoint he studies the manifestations of a split personality, a version of the *Doppelgänger* motif common in nineteenth-century literature. The ironic reversal of roles appears at first to be a harmless joke, but Andersen convincingly depicts how the subconscious can subdue both conscience and consciousness. The final effect is a chilling picture of those dark and irrational undercurrents in human experience that continue to surface no matter how people try to repress them.

There is also another significant aspect to the "chilling effect" of the tale that pertains to the ethical role of the artist and art. Clayton Koelb points to this feature in his insightful essay, "The Rhetoric of Ethical Engagement":

> There is no doubt that "The Shadow" operates on one level at least as a melancholy allegory of the relationship between an artist and his work of art. Andersen takes the traditional notion that an artist's works are his "offspring," capable of living on after he is dead, and turns upon it an almost Freudian suspicion. The more successful a work of art is, the more he puts its creator "in the shade."... That Andersen cast in the role of protagonist a transparent double of himself adds to the grim irony of the parable."[31]

In essence, the story reveals a process by which an author becomes eclipsed and eliminated by his very own works. There is thus a "shady" side to artistic production, for the artworks that survive the artist may do damage by revealing secrets that harm people and the artist himself.

Written in 1847, "The Shadow" shows Andersen at the height of his powers as a fairy-tale writer. By now confident in his art so that he could also show how his art might master him, he no longer confined himself to writing stories seemingly for children, and he exploited all types of sources and material for his tales, not just folklore. The length and style of the tales vary considerably. Some are a few pages in length, others are over thirty pages. Some are overly didactic and sentimental; others are ironic, complex, and bitter.

In "A Drop of Water" (1848) Andersen creates a philosophical allegory based on social Darwinism to convey a sardonic view of the cutthroat life and class struggles in Copenhagen. "The Story of a Mother" (1848) is a slightly veiled rendition of his mother's life and the trials and tribulations she endured. "There Is a Difference" (1855) concerns a dispute between a haughty apple tree and a common dandelion, Andersen's point being that both are children of beauty blessed by God. "Everything in Its Right Place" (1853) and "The Pixy at the Grocer's" (1853) are political fantasy narratives that illustrate the influence of the 1848–50 revolution on Andersen. In the first story he depicts the rise to power of diligent, hardworking peasants and middle-class people over the aristocracy. In the other he pokes fun at a pixy who cannot make up his mind whether to fight for his ideals or to make a compromise with a grocer so he can have bread and security. Such is Andersen's metaphorical comment on people as reluctant revolutionaries.

"Lovely" (1859) is a brilliant satire on sentimental love and the false appreciation of art. Here a young sculptor is deceived by the outward appearance of a beautiful woman, marries her, and leads a banal life until her death frees him to pursue true art. "On the Last Day" (1852) is a short religious tract about the immortality of the soul. In "The Two Maidens" (1861) Andersen plays superbly with a change in the Danish language concerning gender to comment on the prospects of female emancipation. "The Puppeteer" (1861) is a fantasy story in which the dream of a puppeteer becomes a nightmare when he must contend with conceited actors in a theater instead of with his dolls. In "The Dung Beetle" (1861) Andersen uses the fable form to write a humorous self-parody. A conceited beetle rises from a dung heap, travels around the world, and mistakenly believes he is honored everywhere without realizing how foolish and pompous he is. "In the Duckyard" (1861) is also a satirical parable, but here Andersen is concerned with attacking the pettiness and arrogance of Danish critics.

His more positive ideas about literature are elaborated in the philosophical piece "The Muse of the Twentieth Century" (1861), in which he argues that poetry can benefit from the inventions of the modern industrial world — ideas that correspond to his essay "Poetry's California." Such optimism is modified in "The Snail and the Rosebush" (1861), a Socratic dialogue in which cynicism is matched against creative naiveté. In an amusing realistic anecdote, "Auntie" (1866), Andersen portrays an eccentric spinster obsessed with the theater, and he uses the occasion to reflect on the fanatic nature of theatergoers and practitioners.

"The Rags" (1868) is another of Andersen's amusing allegorical dialogues; two rags, one Norwegian and one Danish, assert the virtues of their respective cultures. When they are made into paper, their claims to greatness are gently mocked. The Norwegian rag becomes a piece of stationery on which a young Norwegian writes a love letter to a Danish girl, while the Danish rag becomes a sheet of paper on which a Danish poet composes an ode in praise of the loveliness and strength of Norway. "The Cripple" (1872), one of Andersen's final commentaries on art, is a fairy tale within a fairy tale about the social and moral value of the genre.

A bedridden cripple named Hans reads tales to his parents, who reject them as worthless. Gradually, however, the adults learn to broaden their horizons and appreciate life through the stories. Hans himself makes a miraculous recovery because of them. Aided by the book of tales and the patronage of the rich family that has given it to him, he makes his way through life as one of Andersen's typical Aladdin figures.

The foregoing summary of Andersen's late and neglected tales can only indicate the broad spectrum of his interests. Many of these stories and others fall flat because they are obvious diatribes or homilies, blunt or quaint. But the best fuse the tensions of his personal experience with folklore and literary motifs to create vivid symbolic narratives that can be appreciated and interpreted in manifold ways. Two works from his late period worth discussing in more detail are "The Ice Maiden" (1861) and "The Gardener and His Master" (1871); both represent major tendencies in his work. "The Ice Maiden" comes from a legend that inspired Johann Peter Hebel to write "Unverhofftes Wiedersehen" ("The Unanticipated Reencounter," 1811) and E. T. A. Hoffmann to create "Die Bergwerke zu Falun" (The Mines of Falun, 1819). Based on an actual event, the original story concerns a man who disappears on his wedding day and is found petrified in stone many years later. Hebel retold the story as a short, vividly realistic anecdote. Hoffmann expanded and transformed it into a mysterious, romantic fairy tale about a young man who must decide whether he will serve the queen of crystals in the underworld, which represents erotic and seductive art, or whether he will marry the wholesome daughter of a miner, who represents solid and virtuous middle-class life. Torn between two worlds, the young man ultimately disappears and dies in the mines. Many years later he is found and reunited with his wife in death. This theme is also touched on by Tieck in "Der Runenberg" (1802), and because Andersen was drawn to the German romantics, it is no wonder that he, too, was captivated by this story. Composed in fifteen chapters, "The Ice Maiden" is one of Andersen's longer tales directed at both children and adults. The setting is Switzerland, which Andersen had recently visited. His hero is a young, talented orphan named Rudy, who escapes the clutches of the Ice Maiden after she kills his mother. But she threatens to catch him too (p. 739):

> Mine is the power!… I crush anything that comes within my grasp and never let it go! A lovely boy was stolen from me. I had kissed him but not so hard that he died from it. Now he is

again among human beings. He herds goats in the mountains. Upward, ever upward, he climbs, away from everyone else, but not from me. He is mine and I claim him.

While the Ice Maiden pursues Rudy single-mindedly, he pursues his destiny and becomes the most skilled hunter and mountain climber in the region. Moreover, his noble character and perseverance enable him to win the hand of Babette, the daughter of a rich miller. On the day before their wedding, however, Rudy drowns while trying to retrieve a rowboat that has drifted from the island where he and Babette had been spending a quiet afternoon. The Ice Maiden was waiting for him and pulled him under. Babette, who had previously had a warning vision of their married life and of a sin committed against Rudy and God, is relieved by his death, since it will prevent her from committing this sin. She spends the rest of her life alone, and Andersen ends his bittersweet tale by describing her situation as follows: "The snow on the mountainside has a rose luster, and so does the heart who believes that 'God wills the best for us all.' But few are so fortunate as Babette, who had it revealed to her in a dream" (p. 781).

Unlike the romantics, Andersen is not concerned with the problem of art and the artist in this story. Nor does he argue that society is too philistine and destructive for the creative artist, who must either devote himself to art or die. Andersen takes a more conservative position. He portrays the struggles of a poor, gifted boy who prospers because he is receptive to the natural wonders of divine creation. Such was Andersen's customary self-depiction in fictional form. Genius can be found in the lower classes, and given the proper conditions, it can flourish. Rudy's "nobility" is glorified, but Andersen also added a melodramatic ending that reflected his attitude toward unobtainable women, unrequited love, and Christian salvation.

Through careful description of the Swiss locale and humorous sketches of the miller's household, Andersen transforms the common events and everyday routine of country people into a miraculous adventure story. Despite the unhappy ending, Andersen sought to convince his readers that everyone is actually fortunate because God's intentions are good. The religious and utopian elements of his thinking endow the tale with its powerful social appeal. Miracles can occur. The rise from rags to riches in accord with God's will is possible. Even though evil lurks in the world in the form of the Ice Maiden, spiritual happiness cannot be denied if one is true to one's God-given gifts.

This was Andersen's optimistic outlook. Yet he was also somewhat skeptical as to whether true genius could receive its just reward or be entirely happy, especially in Denmark. In one of his saddest and finest tales, "The Gardener and His Master," written toward the end of his life, this skepticism is given full expression. The story is sad because it indicates that Andersen still felt unrecognized and unappreciated at the end of his life. It is fine because it is a subtle critique of the upper classes and their incapability of evaluating genuine art. Andersen portrays a gifted gardener whose fruit and flowers make him renowned throughout the country, but his own employers cannot see how he fertilizes their soil to produce beautiful plants. In fact, they have no idea how rich their own soil is because they are so prejudiced against their own common stock. The gardener clearly symbolizes the talented artist who can take ordinary soil and transform it into something extraordinary. Andersen prided himself on performing such "magical" feats, but he was disturbed by the lack of appreciation exhibited by the upper classes and intelligentsia in Denmark. Was this a common problem that all artists faced? Must all true artists endure jealousy and arrogance? Are artists who come from the lower classes the only ones faced with such despicable treatment?

Andersen pondered these questions time and again and presented them in different symbolic forms, as though he hoped his private problems as a "common" artist blessed with genius might be resolved through his different approaches. The result is an immense, rich canon of fairy tales that reflects the social situation of art and the artist as well as social injustices in the nineteenth century. Andersen tried desperately to give his life the form and content of a fairy tale, precisely because he was a troubled, lonely, and highly neurotic artist who sublimated in literary creation his failure to fulfill his wishes and dreams in reality. His literary fame rests on this failure, for what he was unable to achieve for himself he created for millions of readers, young and old, with the hope that their lives might be different from his. Ironically, to read the fairy tales of Andersen today and gain hope means that we must understand the despair of the writer, whom we no longer neglect as we probe the disquieting features in his life and work.

The Discourse of the Dominated

Andersen visited me here several years ago. He seemed to me
like a tailor. This is the way he really looks. He is a haggard man
with a hollow, sunken face, and his demeanor betrays an anxious,
devout type of behavior that kings love. This is the reason why
they give Andersen such a brilliant reception. He is the perfect
representation of all poets, just the way kings want them to be.

Heinrich Heine (1851)[1]

Andersen's Essentialism

If the Grimm brothers were the first writers in the nineteenth century to
distinguish themselves by remodeling oral folk tales explicitly for a bourgeois socialization process, then Hans Christian Andersen completed
their mission, creating, between 1835 and 1874, a canon of literary fairy
tales in praise of essentialist ideology for children and adults. By infusing
his tales with general notions of the Protestant ethic and essentialist ideas
of natural biological order, Andersen was able to receive the bourgeois
seal of good housekeeping. From the dominant-class point of view, his
tales were deemed useful and worthy enough for rearing children of all
classes, and they became a literary staple in Western culture. Niels Kofoed
has underlined that Andersen had basically one tale to tell, not unlike the
Horatio Alger myth, and he repeated it so persuasively and charmingly
that it was embraced by the imagination of nineteenth-century readers:

> Andersen, identifying with Aladdin, made his tale a leitmotif
> in the drama of his own life. When people would mock him for
> his peculiar appearance, he would clench his fists in his pockets
> saying: I am going to prove that I am not the simpleton that

47

they take me for! Just wait! Some day they will stand up and bow to the triumphant poet — the genius of the world, who will be seated on Parnassus beside Homer, Dante, Shakespeare and Goethe. Andersen told this tale time and again.... In Andersen's novels and in his tales and stories he repeated and varied the theme of his life numerous times, developing it and enlarging on it, turning it into a universal song about poetry being of common interest to all mankind. He even considered the fairy-tale genre to be the underlying structure of all good novels and the universal genre of a coming global civilization.[2]

Fortunately for Andersen, he appeared on the scene when the original middle-class prejudice against imaginative fairy tales was receding. In fact, there was gradual recognition that fantasy could be employed for the utilitarian needs of the bourgeoisie, and Andersen proved to be a most humble servant in this cause.

But what was at the heart of Andersen's mode of service? In what capacity did his tales serve children and adults in Europe and America? What is the connection between Andersen's achievement as a fairy-tale writer, his servile demeanor, and our cultural appreciation of his tales? It seems to me that these questions have to be posed even more critically if we are to understand the underlying reasons behind Andersen's rise to fame and general acceptance in the nineteenth century. In fact, they are crucial if we want to grasp the continual reception, service, and use of the tales in the twenty-first century, particularly in regard to socialization through literature and film.

Despite the fact that Andersen wrote a great deal about himself and his tales and was followed by scholars who have investigated every nook and cranny of his life and work, there have been very few attempts to study his tales ideologically and to analyze their function in the acculturation process. This is all the more surprising when one considers that they were written with a plump didactic purpose and were overloaded with references to normative behavior and ideal political standards. Indeed, the discourse of his narratives has a distinct ideological bias peculiarly "marred" by his ambivalent feelings toward his social origins and the dominant classes in Denmark that controlled his fortunes. It is this "marred ambivalence" that is subsumed in his tales and lends them their dynamic tension. Desirous of indicating the way to salvation through emulation of the upper classes and of paying reverence to the Protestant ethic, Andersen also showed that this path was filled with suffering, humiliation, and torture — and that it could even lead to crucifixion. It is because of his ambivalent attitude, particularly toward the dominance of essentialist ideology, that his tales have retained their basic appeal up through the present day. But before we reevaluate this appeal as constituted by the socializing elements of the tales, we must first turn to reconsider Andersen in light of the class conflict and conditions of social assimilation in his day.

As we have seen in the previous chapter, the more Andersen succeeded in high society, the more he became ashamed that he was the son of a poor cobbler and a washerwoman. Embarrassed by his proletarian background, he grew to insist on notions of natural nobility. Once he became a successful writer, he rarely mingled with the lower classes. If anything, the opposite was the case: he was known to ingratiate himself by making amusing paper cuts and performing for his dinner, so to speak, before upper-class families that he visited in Copenhagen and throughout all of Europe. Indeed, he successfully opened doors that had been shut in his face when he had first arrived in Copenhagen, and he made himself welcome by learning how to alter his bearing to please his so-called superiors. However, his success then and now cannot be attributed to his opportunism and conformism. That is, he cannot simply be dismissed as a class renegade who catered to the aesthetic and ideological interests of the dominant classes. His case is much more complex, for in many respects his tales were innovative narratives that explored the limits of assimilation in a closed social order to which he aspired. Despite all the recognition and acceptance by the nobility and bourgeoisie in the Western world, Andersen never felt himself to be a full-fledged member of any group. He was the outsider, the loner, who constantly traveled in his mature years, and his wanderings were symptomatic (as the wanderers and birds in his tales) of a man who hated to be dominated, though he loved the dominant class.

As Elias Bredsdorff, one of the more astute biographers of Andersen, maintains:

> Speaking in modern terms Andersen was a man born in the "Lumpenproletariat" but completely devoid of class "consciousness." In his novels and tales he often expresses an unambiguous sympathy for "the underdog," especially for people who have been deprived of their chance of success because of their humble

origins, and he pours scorn on haughty people who pride themselves on their noble birth or their wealth and who despise others
for belonging to, or having their origin in, the lower classes. But
in his private life Andersen accepted the system of absolutism
and its inherent class structure, regarded royalty with awe and
admiration and found a special pleasure in being accepted by
and associating with kings, dukes and princes, and the nobility
at home and abroad.[3]

Though Andersen's sympathy did lay with the downtrodden and disenfranchised in his tales, it was not as unambiguous as Bredsdorff would
have us believe, for Andersen's fawning servility to the upper classes
also manifested itself in his fiction. In fact, as I have maintained, the
ambivalent feelings about both his origins and the nobility constitute the
appeal of the tales. Andersen prided himself on his "innate" gifts as poet
(*Digter*), and he devoutly believed that certain biologically determined
people were chosen by divine providence to rise above others. This belief
was his rationalization for aspiring toward recognition and acceptance
by the upper classes. And here an important distinction must be made.
More than anything else, Andersen sought the blessing and recognition of Jonas Collin and the other members of this respectable, wealthy,
patriarchal family as well as other people from the educated bureaucratic
class in Denmark like Henriette (Jette) Wulff. In other words, Andersen
endeavored to appeal to the Danish bourgeois elite — cultivated in the
arts, adept at commerce and administration, and quick to replace the
feudal caste of aristocrats as the leaders of Denmark.

The relationship to Jonas Collin was crucial in his development, for
Collin took him in hand, when he came to Copenhagen, and practically
adopted him as a son. At first he tried to make a respectable bourgeois
citizen out of the ambitious "poet," but he gradually relented and supported Andersen's artistic undertakings. In due course, Andersen's primary
audience came to be the Collin family and people with similar attitudes.
All his artistic efforts throughout his life were aimed at pleasing them.
For instance, on Jonas Collin's birthday in 1845 he wrote the following:

> You know that my greatest vanity, or call it rather joy, consists
> in making you realize that I am worthy of you. All the kind
> of appreciation I get makes me think of you. I am truly
> popular, truly appreciated abroad, I am famous — all right,
> you're smiling. But the cream of the nations fly towards me,

I find myself accepted in all families, the greatest compliments are paid to me by princes and by the most gifted of men. You should see the way people in so-called High Society gather ro und me. Oh, no one at home thinks of this among the many who entirely ignore me and might be happy to enjoy even a drop of the homage paid to me. My writings must have greater value than the Danes will allow for. Heiberg has been translated too, but no one speaks of his work, and it would have been strange if the Danes were the only ones to be able to make judgments in this world. You must know, you my beloved father must understand that you did not misjudge me when you accepted me as your son, when you helped and protected me.[4]

Just as important as his relationship to the father Collin was his relationship to his "adopted" brother Edvard, who served as Andersen's superego and most severe critic. Not only did Edvard edit Andersen's manuscripts and scold him for writing too fast and too much to gain fame, but he set standards of propriety for the writer through his cool reserve, social composure, and businesslike efficiency. In his person, Edvard Collin — a Danish legal administrator like his father — represented everything Andersen desired to become, and Andersen developed a strong homo-erotic attachment to Edvard that remained visibly powerful during his life. In 1838 Andersen wrote a revealing letter that indicates just how deep his feelings for Edvard were:

I'm longing for you, indeed, at this moment I'm longing for you as if you were a lovely Calabrian girl with dark blue eyes and a glance of passionate flames. I've never had a brother, but if I had I could not have loved him the way I love you, and yet — you do not reciprocate my feelings! This affects me painfully or maybe this is in fact what binds me even more firmly to you. My soul is proud, the soul of a prince cannot be prouder. I have clung to you, I have — bastare! which is a good Italian verb to be translated in Copenhagen as "shut up!"... Oh, I wish to God that you were poor and I rich, distinguished, a nobleman. In that case I should initiate you into the mysteries, and you would appreciate me more than you do now. Oh! If there is an eternal life, as indeed there must be, then we shall truly understand and appreciate one another. Then I shall no longer be the poor person in need of kind interest and friends, then we shall be equal.[5]

The fact is that Andersen never felt himself equal to any of the Collins, and he measured his worth by the standards they set. Their letters to him prescribe humility, moderation, asceticism, decorum, economy of mind and soul, devotion to God, and loyalty to Denmark. On the one hand, the Collin family provided Andersen with a home, and on the other, their criticism and sobriety made him feel insecure. They were too classical and refined, too "grammatically" correct, and he knew he could never achieve full recognition as a *Digter* in their minds. Yet that realization did not stop him from trying to prove his moral worth and aesthetic talents to them in his tales and novels. This is not to suggest that all or even most of the fairy tales are totally informed by Andersen's relationship with the Collins. However, to understand their vital aspect — the ideological formation in relationship to the linguistic and semantic discourse — it is important to grasp how Andersen approached and worked through notions of social domination.

Here Noëlle Bisseret's study, *Education, Class Language and Ideology*, is most useful for my purposes because she endeavors to understand the historical origins of essentialist ideology and the concepts of natural aptitudes that figure prominently in Andersen's tales. According to her definition:

> Essentialist ideology, which originates along with the establishment of those structures constituting class societies, is a denial of the historical relations of an economic, political, juridical and ideological order which preside over the establishment of labile power relationships. Essentialist ideology bases all social hierarchy on the transcendental principle of a natural biological order (which took over from a divine principle at the end of the eighteenth century). A difference in essence among human beings supposedly predetermines the diversity of a psychic and mental phenomena ("intelligence," "language," etc.) and thus the place of an individual in a social order considered as immutable.[6]

By analyzing how the concepts of aptitude and disposition were used to designate a contingent reality in the late feudal period, Bisseret is able to show a transformation in meaning to legitimize the emerging power of the bourgeoisie in the nineteenth century: aptitude becomes an essential hereditary feature and is employed to justify social inequalities. In other words, the principle of equality developed by the bourgeoisie was gradually employed as a socializing agent to demonstrate that there are certain select people in a free market system, people with innate talents who are destined to succeed and rule because they "possess or own" the essential qualities of intelligence, diligence, and responsibility.

We must remember that the nineteenth century was the period in which the interest in biology, eugenics, and race became exceedingly strong.[7] Not only did Charles Darwin and Herbert Spencer elaborate their theories at this time, but Arthur de Gobineau wrote his *Essai sur l'inegalité des races humaines* (1852) and Francis Galton wrote *Hereditary Genius* (1869) to give a seemingly scientific veneer to the middle-class social selection process. Throughout the Western world, a more solidified bourgeois public sphere was establishing itself and replacing feudal systems, as was clearly the case in Denmark.[8] Along with the new institutions designed for rationalization and maximization of profit, a panoptic principle of control, discipline, and punishment was introduced into the institutions of socialization geared to enforce the interests and to guarantee the domination of the propertied classes. This is fully demonstrated in Michel Foucault's valuable study *Discipline and Punish*,[9] which supports Bisseret's thesis of how the ideological concept of attitudes became the "scientific" warrant of a social organization which it justified:

> The ideology of natural inequalities conceived and promoted by a social class at a time when it took economic, and later on political, power gradually turned into a scientific truth, borrowing from craniometry, then from anthropometry, biology, genetics, psychology, and sociology (the scientific practice of which it sometimes oriented) the elements enabling it to substantiate its assertions. And by this very means, it was able to impose itself upon all the social groups which believed in the values presiding over the birth of aptitude as an ideology: namely Progress and Science. It now appears that well beyond the controversies, which oppose the different established groups, this general ideology directs the whole conception of selection and educational guidance: the educational system aims at selecting and training an "elite," which by its competence, merit, and aptitude is destined for high functions, the responsibility of which entails certain social and economic advantages.[10]

If we look at the case of Andersen in light of Bisseret's thesis at this point, two factors are crucial for his personal conception of an essentialist ideology.

First, Denmark was a tiny country with a tightly knit bureaucratic feudal structure that was rapidly undergoing a transformation into a bourgeois-dominated society. There were fewer than 1,200,000 people in the country, and 120,000 in Copenhagen. Among the educated bourgeoisie and nobility, everyone knew everyone else who was of importance, and, though the country depended on the bourgeois bureaucratic administrators and commercial investors, the king and his advisers made most of the significant decisions up until the early 1840s, when constitutive assemblies representing the combined interests of industry, commerce, and agriculture began assuming more control. Essentially, as Bredsdorff has aptly stated, "in Danish society of the early nineteenth century it was almost impossible to break through class barriers. Almost the only exceptions were a few individuals with unusual artistic gifts: Bertel Thorvaldsen, Fru Heiberg, and Hans Christian Andersen. And even they had occasionally to be put in their place and reminded of their low origin."[11] Here it is difficult to talk about a real breakthrough. Throughout his life Andersen was obliged to act as a dominated subject within the dominant social circles despite his fame and recognition as a writer.

Even to reach this point — and this is the second crucial factor — he had to be strictly supervised, for admission to the upper echelons had to be earned and constantly proved. And, Andersen appeared to be a "security risk" at first. Thus, when he came to Copenhagen in 1819 from the lower-class and provincial milieu of Odense, he had to be corrected by his betters so that he could cultivate proper speech, behavior, and decorum. Then for polishing he was also sent to elite private schools in Slagelse and Helsingör at a late age from 1822 to 1827 to receive a thorough formal and classical education. The aim of this education was to curb and control Andersen, especially his flamboyant imagination, and not to help him achieve a relative amount of autonomy:

> Jonas Collin's purpose in rescuing Andersen and sending him to a grammar school was not to make a great writer out of him but to enable him to become a useful member of the community in a social class higher than the one into which he was born. The grammar-school system was devised to teach boys to learn properly, to mould them into the desired finished products, to make them grow up to be like their fathers.[12]

As Bredsdorff remarks, the system was not so thorough that Andersen was completely reshaped and stamped for complete approval. But it left its indelible marks. What Andersen was to entitle *The Fairy Tale of My Life* — his autobiography, a remarkable mythopoeic projection of his life[13] — was in actuality a process of self-denial cultivated as individual genius with God-given talents. As I have pointed out, Andersen was ashamed of his family background and did his utmost to avoid talking or writing about it. When he did, he invariably distorted the truth. For him, home was the Collin family, but home, as Andersen knew quite well, was unattainable because of social differences.

It was through his writings and literary achievement that Andersen was able to veil his self-denial and present it as a distinct form of individualism. At the beginning of the nineteenth century in Denmark there was a literary swing from the universality of classicism to the romantic cult of genius and individuality, and Andersen benefited from this greatly. As a voracious reader, Andersen consumed all the German romantic writers of fairy tales along with Shakespeare, Scott, Irving, and other writers who exemplified his ideal of individualism. Most important for his formation in Denmark, as I have already remarked, the romantic movement was:

> accompanied by what is known as the Aladdin motif, after the idea which Oehlenschläger expressed in his play *Aladdin*. This deals with the theory that certain people are chosen by nature, or God, or the gods, to achieve greatness, and that nothing can succeed in stopping them, however weak and ill-suited they may otherwise seem.... The twin themes of former national greatness and of the possibility of being chosen to be great, despite all appearances, assumed a special significance for Denmark after 1814. Romantic-patriotic drama dealing with the heroic past appealed to a population looking for an escape from the sordid present, and served as a source of inspiration for many years. At the same time the Aladdin conception also took on new proportions: it was not only of use as a literary theme, but it could be applied to individuals — Oehlenschläger felt that he himself exemplified it, as did Hans Christian Andersen — and it was also possible to apply it to a country.[14]

This leads to the concept of Andersen as Aladdin, or of Andersen's life as a fairy tale. There is something schizophrenic in pretending that one is a fairy-tale character in reality, and Andersen was indeed troubled by nervous disorders and psychic disturbances throughout his life. As noted in Chapter 1, Andersen developed a very peculiar religious and philosophical belief system — based on ideas presented by the Danish physicist Hans Christian Ørsted in *The Spirit of Nature* (1850) — to temper his compulsive drive for success and thirst for admiration. To justify his "schizophrenic" existence, he adopted Ørsted's ideas and combined them with his animistic belief in Christianity.[15] Both Andersen and Ørsted were followers of the theory of intelligent design. Therefore, if the great Creator controlled the workings of the world, genius was a divine and natural gift and would be rewarded regardless of birth. Power was located in the hands of God, and only before Him did one have to bow. However, Andersen did in fact submit more to a temporal social system and had to rationalize this submission adequately enough so that he could live with himself. In doing so, he inserted himself into a sociohistorical nexus of the dominated denying his origins and needs to receive applause, money, comfort, and space to write about social contradictions that he had difficulty resolving for himself. Such a situation meant a life of self-doubt and anxiety for Andersen.

Again Bisseret is useful in helping us understand the sociopsychological impact on such ego formation and perspectives:

> Dominant in imagination (who am I?), dominated in reality (what am I?), the ego lacks cohesion, hence the contradiction and incoherence of the practices. Dominated-class children think in terms of aptitudes, tastes and interests because at each step in their education their success has progressively convinced them that they are not "less than nothing" intellectually; but at the same time they profoundly doubt themselves. This doubt is certainly not unrelated to the split, discontinuous aspects of their orientations, as measured by the standards of a parsimonious and fleeting time. Their day-to-day projects which lead them into dead ends or which build up gaps in knowledge which are inhibitory for their educational future, reinforce their doubts as to their capacities.[16]

In the particular case of Andersen, the self-doubts were productive insofar as he constantly felt the need to prove himself, to show that his aptitude and disposition were noble and that he belonged to the elect. This is apparent in the referential system built into most of his tales, which are discourses of the dominated. In analyzing such discourse, Bisseret makes the point that:

the relationship to his social being simultaneously lived and conceived by each agent is based on unconscious knowledge. What is designated as the "subject" (the "I") in the social discourse is the social being of the dominant. Thus in defining his identity the dominated cannot polarize the comparison between the self/the others on his "me" in the way the dominant does.... There cannot be a cohesion except on the side of power. Perhaps the dominated ignore that less than the dominant, as is clear through their accounts. Indeed, the more the practices of the speaker are the practices of power, the more the situation in which he places himself in the conceptual field is the mythical place where power disappears to the benefit of a purely abstract creativity. On the other hand, the more the speaker is subjected to power, the more he situates himself to the very place where power is concretely exercised.[17]

Though Bisseret's ideas about the dominated and dominant in regard to essentialist ideology are concerned with linguistic forms in everyday speech, they also apply to modes of narration used by writers of fiction. For instance, Andersen mixed popular language or folk linguistic forms with formal classical speech in creating his tales, and this stylistic synthesis not only endowed the stories with an unusual tone but also reflected Andersen's efforts to unify an identity that dominant discourse kept dissociating. Andersen also endeavored to ennoble and synthesize folk motifs with the literary motifs of romantic fairy tales, particularly those of E. T. A. Hoffmann, Ludwig Tieck, Adalbert von Chamisso, Joseph von Eichendorff, and Friedrich de La Motte-Fouqué. His stylization of lower-class folk motifs was similar to his personal attempt to rise in society: they were aimed at meeting the standards of "high art" set by the middle classes. As Bengt Holbek points out in regard to Andersen's use of folk tales, "He heard them in one milieu and told them in another. He had to make adjustments, one of which was that he had to disguise or obliterate all traces of overt sexuality; such matters were not then deemed fitting entertainment for the children of the bourgeoisie."[18] The self-censorship was done in accordance with the principles of domination, but it was also undermined by Andersen's own metaphorical language that exposed his contradictions. In sum, Andersen's linguistic forms and stylized motifs reveal the structure of relationships as they were being formed and solidified around emerging bourgeois domination in the nineteenth century.

With a few exceptions, most of the 156 fairy tales written by Andersen contain no "I," that is, the "I" is sublimated through the third person, and the narrative discourse becomes dominated by constant reference to the location of power. The identification of the third-person narrator with the underdog or dominated in the tales is consequently misleading. On one level, this occurs, but the narrator's voice always seeks approval and identification with a higher force. Here, too, the figures representing dominance or nobility are not always at the seat of power. Submission to power beyond the aristocracy constituted and constitutes the real appeal of Andersen's tales for middle-class audiences: Andersen placed power in divine providence, which invariably acted in the name of bourgeois essentialist ideology. No other writer of literary fairy tales in the early nineteenth century introduced so many Christian notions of God, the Protestant ethic, and bourgeois enterprise in his narratives as Andersen did. All his tales make explicit or implicit reference to a miraculous Christian power that rules firmly but justly over His subjects. Such patriarchal power would appear to represent a feudal organization, but the dominant value system represented by providential action and the plots of the tales is thoroughly bourgeois and justifies essentialist notions of aptitude and disposition. Just as aristocratic power was being transformed in Denmark, so Andersen reflected upon the meaning of such transformation in his tales.

There are also clear strains of social Darwinism mixed with the Aladdin motif in Andersen's tales. In fact, survival of the fittest is the message of the very first tale he wrote for the publication of his anthology — "The Tinderbox." However, the fittest is not always the strongest but, rather, is the chosen protagonist who proves himself or herself worthy of serving a dominant value system. This does not mean that Andersen constantly preached one message in all his tales. As a whole, written from 1835 to 1874, they represent the creative process of a dominated ego endeavoring to establish a unified self while confronted with a dominant discourse, which dissociated this identity. The fictional efforts are variations on a theme of how to achieve approbation, assimilation, and integration in a social system that does not allow for real acceptance or recognition if one comes from the lower classes. In many respects, Andersen is like a Humpty-Dumpty figure who had a great fall when he realized as he grew up that entrance into the educated elite of Denmark did not mean acceptance and totality. Nor could all the king's men and horses put him back together when he perceived the inequalities and was humiliated. So his fairy tales are variegated and sublimated efforts to achieve wholeness, to gain vengeance, and to depict the reality of class struggle. The dominated voice, however, remains constant in its reference to real power.

Obviously there are other themes than power and domination in the tales and other valid approaches to them, but I believe that the widespread, continuous reception of Andersen's fairy tales in Western culture can best be explained by understanding how the discourse of the dominated functions in the narratives. Ideologically speaking, Andersen furthered bourgeois notions of the self-made man or the Horatio Alger myth, which was becoming very popular in America and elsewhere, while reinforcing a belief in the existing power structure that meant domination and exploitation of the lower classes. Indeed, Andersen's fame in America and England in the nineteenth century was somewhat meteoric. This is why we must look more closely at the tales to analyze how they embody the dreams of social rise and individual happiness that further a powerful, all-encompassing bourgeois selection process furthering domination of the mind and fantasy.

Individual Happiness and Domination of the Mind

Most scholars of Andersen's tales note that he initially published his tales for children and gradually shifted his attention to adults. Actually, he always wrote for adults, and his tales began to exclude children as readers after 1850. The first booklets, called *Eventyr, fortalte for Børn* (*Fairy Tales Told for Children*), were published as insets in books for adults in 1837. Gradually the booklets became books for children, with illustrations by Vilhelm Pedersen. Then changes were made in the titles to *Eventyr* (*Fairy tales*), *Nye Eventyr* (*New Fairy Tales*), *Historier* (*Stories*), and finally by 1850, *Eventyr og Historier* (*Fairy Tales and Stories*). The evolution of his style and interests are reflected in the titles of the volumes and his shift of focus. Andersen began first by transforming tales from the oral tradition and adapting them for bourgeois children and adults. By the early 1840s he very rarely used recognizable folk tales as his subject matter but created more and more his very own fairy tales by animating plants, animals, and things — something that he had done from the very beginning. But now the preponderance of the tales dealt with animals and objects in narratives that resembled fables and parables but were mixed with motifs from fairy tales. Finally, after 1850 his tales were no longer addressed to children and included legends, philosophical ruminations, supernatural stories, and historical commentaries. As Mortensen has commented:

Like all great artists Andersen struggled first and foremost with himself by continually widening the bounds of his expressive abilities. This is exemplified in his unrequited love of the theater and in his attempts to expand the shorter prose of the fairy tale to epic compositions. Today many of these attempts are forgotten because there was a limit to what could be successful — even for Andersen. The core of his mastery of the fairy tale, however, lies in his lucid detailed observations, in his ability to perceive the odd aspects of existence, and in the tightly composed world of the short prose works which, in a concise oral language, reveal the schism in the uniform bourgeois culture within which, and against which, tales are written.[19]

While Mortensen argues that each one of Andersen's tales should be analyzed and interpreted carefully as a separate work of art instead of being grouped together and examined as representative of a common or typical Andersen tale, he does see common threads that connect the disparate narratives. One of the most important is the manner in which Andersen revealed "the schism in the uniform bourgeois culture" that he almost obsequiously sought to repair throughout his life. The most common thread is his discourse of the dominated, and I want to examine several tales — "The Traveling Companion" (1837), "The Nightingale" (1843), "The Ugly Duckling" (1843), "The Shepherdess and the Chimney Sweep," (1845), "Everything in Its Right Place" (1853), "The Pixy at the Grocer's" (1853), and "The Gardener and His Master" (1871) — to demonstrate how Andersen consistently rationalized the power of dominant groups that distressed and disturbed him. These tales are important because they cover the spectrum of his productive life and reveal how he put his extraordinary talent to use by inventing a variety of approaches to questions that involved the significance of providence, the essence of geniality, the role of the artist, the treatment of women, and the system of patronage.

"The Traveling Companion" is a good example of how Andersen carefully reshaped oral folk tales to suit the religious tastes of a bourgeois readership and to foster his notion of essentialist ideology. It is also a tale that puts women in their proper place and exalts a lowly hero, who is a devout believer in divine providence. In 1830 he wrote an earlier version, "The Dead Man: A Tale from Funen," which was the first tale that he had ever published, but he was not satisfied with it and rewrote it seven years later

The Traveling Companion (1887) illustrated by Joseph J. Mora in *Hans Andersen's Fairy Tales*

as "The Traveling Companion." The material for the tale was well known not only in Denmark but throughout Europe. The Brothers Grimm published a version titled "The Grateful Dead Man and the Princess Rescued from Slavery" in their annotations of 1856, and there were many other variants in circulation before Andersen and the Grimms dealt with this type of tale. In fact, folklorists have traced its history to an oral tradition that existed in the second century B.C. and formed part of the apocryphal book of Tobbit.[20] Antti Aarne and Stith Thompson categorized the different variants under the numbers AT 505–508 "The Grateful Dead"[21] and provided the basic motifs for the tale: The hero comes upon a dead man whose corpse is lying in the open and is being disgraced because the dead man has not paid his debts. The hero shows compassion and pays the debts by giving away all the money he has in his possession. He continues on his way and meets an old man, servant, or fox, who agrees to help him in some quest, provided that he will share his winnings. Now the young man travels with a companion who helps him rescue a princess or helps him free her from a spell. In the end the helper reveals himself as the dead man whose debts the hero had paid and then disappears. In many Scandinavian versions the princess is in league with a troll, who has enchanted her. The hero chops off the head of the troll, and then the princess is whipped with birch switches and bathed three times with milk, sour milk, and sweet milk so that she is purified and can marry the hero.

It is not certain what version Andersen knew, but it is more than likely that he was familiar with a Scandinavian pagan tale, which he completely transformed into a sentimental romantic tale that celebrates the power of God, for the protagonist is helpless without divine power. The message is overt and repeated several times so that the hero, Johannes, appears to be pathetic. Indeed, at the outset he is an orphan who has just buried his father, and when he looks up at the sun, it reveals to him that his father is begging God to help him so that everything will go well for him. Then Johannes responds, "I will always try to be good.... Then I, too, will go to heaven when I die and see my father again. I will have so much to tell him, and he will teach me about all the beautiful things in heaven, as he taught me about all that is beautiful here on earth. Oh, how wonderful it will be!" (p. 41). And it is indeed wonderful. Johannes sets out into the marvelous world, and when he spends a night in a church, he discovers two wicked men who are about to desecrate a dead man in a coffin because he has not paid his debts. Johannes intervenes and gives the men fifty marks, his entire inheritance. Then he declares: "I can get along without money, I am strong and God will help me" (p. 43). He continues on his way, and when he leaves a forest, a stranger, who becomes his traveling companion, joins him. This stranger is not your ordinary companion, for he helps people in need with a magic salve and receives payment from them — birch switches from an old woman and an old sword from a theater director. In addition, he cuts off the wings of a dead swan with his newly acquired sword. Finally Johannes and the stranger arrive at a city where they hear about a beautiful but terrifying princess. She had proclaimed that whoever proposes to her could win her hand in marriage only if he answered three questions. However, if he failed, he would lose his head, and numerous men had already lost their heads. When Johannes hears this, he exclaims, "What a horrible princess.... She should be switched, that is what she deserves. If I were the old king I would beat her until I drew blood" (p. 48). However, as soon as he sees her, he falls helplessly in love with her and decides to propose to her. Everyone tries to dissuade him, but he is stubborn. The night before his test, he falls asleep at the inn, and the stranger attaches the swan's wings to his back, makes himself invisible, and follows the princess, who flies through the air, to the troll's castle. Along the way he beats her with the birch switches, and once there, he learns the answer to her first question and tells it to Johannes, who uses it the next day to save his life. The stranger helps Johannes two more times and cuts off the troll's head. Then he instructs the young man to dip the princess in a tub and duck her under water three times to rid her of the evil spell. "Johannes prayed to God as he pushed her under the third time; and instantly she changed into the most beautiful princess. She was even lovelier than before; and she thanked him, with tears in her eyes, for having broken the evil spell" (p. 55). Now that the stranger's job is done, he reveals himself as the dead debtor and disappears. Johannes marries the princess and soon takes over the kingdom.

On the surface, it would seem that Andersen's rewriting of the oral folk tale about the grateful debtor is a quaint, charming narrative filled with humorous description and solemn appeals to God Almighty that was appropriate for young Danish children and adult readers. Yet, there are some disturbing aspects that need to be addressed because they are repeated time and again in his other tales and reveal how Andersen was prompt to submit his heroes to high authorities like God and to demean female characters, even though his heroes might worship them. There are clear submissive and misogynistic tones in many of his tales. Women must be put in their place, and all places are ordained either by royalty or by divine powers.

Bengt Holbek, who was one of the leading Danish folklorists of the twentieth century, has incisively pointed out how Andersen changed a folk tale from a tale focused on male oppression to one that actually celebrates domination.

The main event of "The Travelling-Companion" is of course the confrontation with the princess who demands to have three questions answered on pain of death. This is where my analysis of folktales leads me to the conclusion that Andersen does not understand what they really are about; or if he understands it he conceals it in such a way as to make it exceedingly difficult for modern people to understand. At this point, it should be emphasized that in traditional peasant communities, magic tales were principally entertainment for adult people. When they are transplanted to the world of the children of the bourgeoisie, some extremely important aspects are lost as I shall try to explain.[22]

What Holbek explains is that the troll was more than likely a symbolic representation of her father, and that the riddle she poses is an expression of an illicit emotional attachment to her father. In other words, the tale, like other well-known folk tales such as "The Maiden without Hands," reflects the dilemma of a young woman who is being oppressed by her father or under her father's spell. The task of the hero is to replace the father, not to win his approval, as is the case in Andersen's tale. Whether one accepts Holbek's interpretation of the folk tale as one that deals with incest, it is clear that Andersen's tale is a "whitewash" and that the narrative structure and themes deal with the maintenance of virtue and virginity in service to a higher authority. The stranger does all the difficult work in the tale. Johannes's mission in life is to show God how clean, innocent, and pure he is. The princess, who is beaten for her so-called bad behavior, is dipped into a tub until she becomes a white swan. Once she is turned into a virgin again, she and her pure husband can marry. But what has Johannes done to deserve her? What is his accomplishment as a hero? Departing from Holbek's thesis somewhat, is it possible that the princess was having an illicit affair with an outsider, a man, whom she desired? Is her father and the court trying to limit her desire? Johannes acts in the name of virtue by basically following the orders of the stranger, who acts allegedly in God's name. Johannes is essentially good and deserving of reward because he complies with commands from above. If Johannes is to be a model protagonist for young readers, and not only for the young, we must bear in mind that he does nothing but help a dead man and moves through the world as a naïve bumpkin, who resembles Joseph von Eichendorff's simpleton in *Aus dem Leben eines Taugenichts*

(*From the Life of a Ne'er-Do-Well*, 1826), a work which Andersen knew. Johannes has his life legislated for him, and thus he is readily accepted by court society, for he will carry out the laws of domination that satisfies the requisites of a king.

In almost all of Andersen's early tales, he focuses on lower-class or disenfranchised protagonists, who "work" their way up and into society. Their rise is predicated on their proper behavior that must correspond to a higher power, which elects and tests the hero. Though respect is shown for feudal patriarchy, the correct normative behavior reflects the values of the bourgeoisie. If the hero comes from the lower classes, he or she must be humbled, if not humiliated, at one point to test obedience. Thereafter, the natural aptitude of a successful individual will be unveiled through diligence, perseverance, and adherence to an ethical system that legitimizes bourgeois domination. Let me be more specific by focusing on what I consider some other popular tales written after 1837, such as "The Nightingale," "The Ugly Duckling," and "The Shepherdess and the Chimney Sweep."

There are two important factors to bear in mind when considering the reception of these tales in the nineteenth century and the present in regard to the narrative discourse of the dominated. First, as a member of the dominated class, Andersen could only experience dissociation despite entrance into upper-class circles. Obviously this was because he measured his success as a person and artist by standards that were not of his own social group's making. That ultimate power, which judged his efforts and the destiny of his heroes, depended on the organization of hierarchical relations at a time of sociopolitical transformation that was to leave Denmark and most of Europe under the control of the bourgeoisie. This shift in power led Andersen to identify with the emerging middle-class elite, but he did not depict the poor and disenfranchised in a negative way. On the contrary, Andersen assumed a humble, philanthropic stance — the fortunate and gifted are obliged morally and ethically to help the less fortunate. The dominated voice of all his narratives does not condemn his former social class; rather, Andersen loses contact with it by denying the rebellious urges of his class within himself and making compromises that affirmed the rightful domination of the middle-class ethic.

A second factor to consider is the fundamental ambiguity of the dominated discourse in Andersen's tales: this discourse cannot represent the interests of the dominated class; it can only rationalize the power of the dominant class so that this power becomes legitimate and acceptable to those who are powerless. As I have noted before, Andersen depersonalizes his tales by using the third-person stance that appears to universalize his voice. However, this self-denial is a recourse of the dominated, who always carry references and appeal to those forces that control their lives. In Andersen's case, he mystifies power and makes it appear divine. It is striking, when one compares Andersen with other fairy-tale writers of his time, how he constantly appeals to God and the Protestant ethic to justify and sanction the actions and results of his tales. Ironically, to have a soul in Andersen's tales, one must sell one's soul either to the aristocracy or to the bourgeoisie, something he clearly knew and felt. In any case, it was the middle-class moral and social code that guaranteed the success of his protagonists, guaranteed his own social success, and ultimately has guaranteed the successful reception of a select number of his tales to the present — canonical tales chosen consciously and unconsciously to maintain ideological notions that serve principles of domination.

This does not mean that Andersen was always self-denigrating in his tales. He often attacked greed and false pride. What is interesting is that vice is generally associated with the pretentious aristocracy and hardly ever with bourgeois characters. Generally speaking, Andersen celebrated the chosen few from the lower classes who naturally rise to fame, and he punished "overreachers" from the lower echelons or "overbearing people" from the upper classes. Decorum and balance became articles of faith in his philosophical scheme of things. Knowing one's place and duty is to form the principle of cognition. For instance, in "The Swineherd," he delights in depicting the poor manners of a princess who has lost her sense of propriety. Andersen had already parodied the artificiality and pretentiousness of the nobility in "The Tinderbox" and "The Emperor's New Clothes." Similar to the "taming of the shrew" motif in the folk tale "King Thrushbeard," Andersen has the dominant figure of the fickle, proud princess humiliated by the dominated figure of the prince disguised as a swineherd. However, there is no happy end here, for the humor assumes a deadly seriousness when the prince rejects the princess after accomplishing his aim: "'I have come to despise you,' said the prince. 'You did not want an honest prince. You did not appreciate the rose or the nightingale, but you could kiss a swineherd for the sake of a toy. Farewell!'" (p. 197).

The oppositions are clear: honesty vs. falseness, genuine beauty (rose/nightingale) vs. manufactured beauty (toys), nobility of the soul vs. soulless nobility. Moreover, as in many instances, the "evil" protagonist is a woman who has lost control of her passions. Indirectly, Andersen argues that the nobility must adapt to the value system of the emerging bourgeoisie or be locked out of the kingdom of happiness. Without appreciating the beauty and power of genuine leaders — the prince is essentially middle class — the monarchy will collapse.

This theme is at the heart of "The Nightingale," which can also be considered a sophisticated treatise about art, genius, and the role of the artist. The plot involves a series of transformations in power relations and service. First the Chinese emperor, a benevolent patriarch, has the nightingale brought to his castle from the forest. When the chief courtier finds the nightingale, he exclaims: "I had not imagined it would look like that. It looks so common! I think it has lost its color from shyness and out of embarrassment at seeing so many noble people at one time" (p. 205). Because the common-looking bird (an obvious reference to Andersen) possesses an inimitable artistic genius, he is engaged to serve the emperor. The first phase of the dominant-dominated relationship based on bonded servitude is changed into neglect when the emperor is given a jeweled mechanical bird that never tires of singing. So the nightingale escapes and returns to the forest, and eventually the mechanical bird breaks down. Five years later the emperor falls sick and appears to be dying. Out of his own choice, the nightingale returns to him and chases death from his window. Here the relationship of servitude is resumed, with the exception that the nightingale has assumed a different market value: he agrees to be the emperor's songbird forever as long as he can come and go as he pleases. Feudalism has been replaced by a free-market system; yet, the bird/artist is willing to serve loyally and keep the autocrat in power (p. 211):

> And my song shall make you happy and make you thoughtful. I shall sing not only of the good and of the evil that happen around you, and yet are hidden from you. For a little songbird flies far. I visit the poor fisherman's cottage and the peasant's hut, far away from your palace and your court. I love your heart more than your crown, and I feel that the crown has a fragrance of something holy about it. I will come! I will sing for you!

In fact, the nightingale's song is indispensable for the emperor's survival. Andersen appears to be making the argument that genuine poetry (*livspoesi*, the poetry of life) is uniquely in touch with the real life of the common people and is also the source of the emperor's life.

The Little Mermaid (1915) illustrated by Harry Clarke in ***Fairy Tales by Hans Christian Andersen***

As we know, Andersen depended on the patronage of the king of Denmark and other upper-class donors, but he never felt sufficiently esteemed, and he resented the strings attached to the money given to him. Instead of breaking with such patronage, however, the dominated voice of this discourse sought to set new limits in which servitude continues, but with market conditions more tolerable for the servant. Andersen reaffirmed the essentialist ideology of this period by positing that gifted "common" individuals are the pillars of power — naturally in service to the state. Unfortunately, he never bothered to ask why "genius" cannot stand on its own and perhaps unite with like-minded people.

In "The Ugly Duckling," genius also assumes a most awe-inspiring shape, but it cannot fly on its own. This tale has generally been interpreted as a parable of Andersen's own success story because the naturally gifted underdog survives a period of "ugliness" to reveal its innate beauty. Yet, more attention should be placed on the servility of genius and beautiful creatures. Though Andersen continually located real power in social conditions that allowed for the emergence of bourgeois hegemony, he often argued — true to conditions in Denmark — that power was to be dispensed in servitude to appreciative rulers, and naturally these benevolent rulers were supposed to recognize the interests of the bourgeoisie. As we have seen in "The Nightingale," the artist returns to serve royalty after the emperor neglects him. In "The Ugly Duckling," the baby swan is literally chased by coarse lower-class animals from the hen yard. His innate beauty cannot be recognized by such crude specimens, and only after he survives numerous ordeals does he realize his essential greatness. But his self-realization is ambivalent, for right before he perceives his true nature, he wants to kill himself (pp. 223–24):

> I shall fly over to them, those royal birds! And they can hack me to death because I, who am so ugly, dare to approach them! What difference does it make! It is better to be killed by them than to be bitten by the other ducks, and pecked by the hens, and kicked by the girl who tends the henyard; or to suffer through the winter.

Andersen expresses a clear disdain for the common people's lot and explicitly states that to be humiliated by the upper class is worth more than the trials and tribulations one must suffer among the lower classes. And, again, Andersen espouses bourgeois essentialist philosophy when he saves the swan and declares as narrator: "It does not matter that one has been born in the hen yard as long as one has lain in a swan's egg" (p. 224). The fine line between eugenics and racism fades in this story where the once-upon-a-time dominated swan reveals himself to be a tame but noble member of a superior race. The swan does not return "home" but lands in a beautiful garden where he is admired by children, adults, and nature. It appears as though the swan has finally come into his own, but, as usual, there is a hidden reference of power. The swan measures himself by the values and aesthetics set by the "royal" swans and by the proper well-behaved children and people in the beautiful garden. The swans and the beautiful garden are placed in opposition to the ducks and the hen yard. In appealing to the "noble" sentiments of a refined audience and his readers, Andersen reflected a distinct class bias if not classical racist tendencies.

This is also the case in "The Shepherdess and the Chimney Sweep," which is a defense of pure love and a flight from sexuality. Similar to "The Ugly Duckling," this humorous but sad tale depicts the journey into the world by the shepherdess and the chimney sweep because they are afraid their pure love will be contaminated by an amazing carved figure, "a man with a long beard, who had little horns sticking out of his forehead and the legs of a goat" (p. 297). The narrator indicates that the shepherdess and the chimney sweep, who are made of porcelain, belong together, while Mr. Goat-legged Commanding-General-Private-War-Sergeant is made of mahogany and is thus unacceptable as a husband for the shepherdess, despite the fact that he has the approval of the Chinese mandarin, her grandfather, another porcelain figure. Why the chimney sweep does not stand his ground and fight for the shepherdess is unclear. At one point he suggests that he and the shepherdess jump into the potpourri jar and throw salt in the mandarin's eyes. But ultimately he complies with the shepherdess's wish to flee the world of the parlor, where arranged marriages appear to be common, and to go out into the wide world. When confronted by this world, however, she becomes frightened and demands to be taken back to the security of the parlor. Upon their return, they find that the porcelain Chinese mandarin had fallen off the table in pursuit of them and had broken into three pieces. The shepherdess exclaims, "How horrible!... Old Grandfather is broken and it's all our fault! I shan't live through it!" (p. 300). But the chimney sweep responds, "He can be put together again.... Don't carry on so!... All he needs is to be glued and have a rivet put in his neck, and he'll be able to say as many nasty things as he ever did" (p. 300). Indeed, the Chinese mandarin is repaired, but because he cannot nod his head, he can no longer give his consent to the threatening goat-legged figure to marry the shepherdess. So, the narrator informs us that "the two young porcelain lovers stayed together. They blessed the rivet in Grandfather's neck and loved each other until they broke" (p. 301).

The ending to the tale is somewhat bittersweet, and the union of the shepherdess and the chimney sweep is only brought about and secured after the Chinese mandarin is restored to his rightful place, albeit with limited power. The flight from oppression becomes a flight back to submission. Even the chimney sweep recognizes this when he says they could have saved themselves a lot of trouble by staying put. They feel sorry for their oppressor, even though his accident inadvertently prevented the shepherdess from the sexual threat of the dark goat figure. Fortunately, their love can remain pure. The racist implications are not as strong in this tale as they are in "The Ugly Duckling," but it is clear that the goat figure as sexual Pan is a dark threat to their innocent state of being. The narrator appears to mock them in the ambivalent ending, for their wholeness cannot last forever. False harmony tops off real disharmony like a varnish.

The Dissatisfaction of the Dominated Artist

What saves Andersen's tales from simply becoming sentimental homilies (which many of them are) was his extraordinary understanding of how class struggle affected the lives of people in his times, and some tales even contain a forthright criticism of abusive domination — though his critique was always balanced by admiration for the upper classes and a fear of poverty. For instance, there are some exceptional tales that suggest a more rebellious position. Indeed, the dominated discourse is not homogenous or univocal, though it constantly refers to bourgeois power and never seeks to defy it. In 1853, shortly after the revolutionary period of 1848–50 in Europe, Andersen reflected upon the thwarted rebellions in a number of tales, and they are worth discussing because they show more clearly how Andersen wavered when he subjected himself to bourgeois and aristocratic domination.

In "Everything in Its Right Place" (1853), the arrogant aristocratic owner of a manor takes pleasure in pushing a goose girl off a bridge. The peddler, who watches this scene and saves the girl, curses the master by exclaiming, "Everything in its right place" (p. 417). Sure enough, the aristocrat drinks and gambles away the manor in the next six years. The new owner is none other than the peddler, and, of course, he takes the goose girl for his bride and the Bible as his guide. The family prospers for the next hundred years with its motto of "everything in its right place." At this point the narrator introduces us to a parson's son tutoring the humble daughter of the now wealthy, ennobled house. This idealistic tutor discusses the differences between the nobility and bourgeoisie and surprises the modest baroness by stating (pp. 420–1):

> I know it is the fashion of the day — and many a poet dances to that tune to say that everything aristocratic is stupid and bad. They claim that only among the poor — and the lower you descend the better — does pure gold glitter. But that is not my opinion; I think it is wrong, absolutely false reasoning. Among the highest classes one can often observe the most elevated traits.… But where nobility has gone to a man's head and he behaves like an Arabian horse that rears and kicks, just because his blood is pure and he has a degree, there nobility has degenerated. When noblemen sniff the air in a room because a plain citizen has been there and say, "It smells of the street," why then Thespis should exhibit them to the just ridicule of satire.

This degradation is, indeed, what occurs. A cavalier tries to mock the tutor at a music soiree, and the tutor plays a melody on a simple willow flute that suddenly creates a storm, with the wind howling, "Everything in its right place!" In the house and throughout the countryside the wind tosses people about, and social class positions are reversed until the flute cracks and everyone returns to their former place. After this scare, Andersen still warns that "eventually everything is put in its right place. Eternity is long, a lot longer than this story" (p. 423). Such a "revolutionary" tone was uncharacteristic of Andersen, but given the mood of the times, he was prompted time and again in the early 1850s to voice his critique of the upper classes and question not only aristocratic but also bourgeois hegemony.

In "The Pixy and the Grocer" (1853), a little imp lives in a grocer's store and receives a free bowl of porridge and butter each Christmas. The grocer also rents out the garret to a poor student who would rather buy a book of poetry and eat bread for supper instead of cheese. The pixy visits the student in the garret to punish him for calling the grocer a boor with no feeling for poetry. Once in the garret, however, the pixy discovers the beauty and magic of poetry and almost decides to move in with the student. Almost, for he remembers that the student does not have much food, nor can he give him porridge with butter. So he continues to visit the garret from time to time. Then one night a fire on the street threatens to spread to the grocer's house. The grocer and his wife grab their gold and bonds and run out of the house. The student remains calm while the pixy tries to save the most valuable thing in the house — the book of poetry. "Now he finally understood his heart's desire, where his loyalty belonged! But when the fire in the house across the street had been put out, then he thought about it again. 'I will share myself between them,' he said, 'for I cannot leave the grocer altogether. I must stay there for the sake of the porridge.'" "That was quite human," the dominated narrator concludes, "after all, we, too, go to the grocer for the porridge's sake" (p. 427).

This tale is much more ambivalent in its attitude toward domination than "Everything in Its Right Place," which is open-ended and allows for the possibility of future revolutions. Here, Andersen writes more about himself and his own contradictions at the time of an impending upheaval (i.e., fire = revolution). Faced with a choice, the pixy/Andersen leans toward poetry or the lower classes and idealism. But, when the fire subsides, he makes his usual compromise, for he knows where his bread is buttered and power resides. The narrative discourse is ironic, somewhat self-critical, but ultimately rationalizing. Everyone falls in line with the dominant forces that provide food, so why not the pixy? Who is he to be courageous or different? Nothing more is said about the student, nor is there any mention of those who do not make compromises. Andersen makes it appear that servility is most human and understandable. Rarely does he suggest that it is just as human to rebel against inequality and injustice out of need as it is to bow to arbitrary domination.

The tales of 1853 demonstrate that Andersen was not unaware of possibilities for radical change and questioned the conditions of bourgeois/aristocratic hegemony. In one of his most remarkable tales "The Gardener and His Master," written toward the end of his life in 1871, he sums up his views on servitude, domination, and aptitude in his typically terse, ambivalent manner. The plot is simple and familiar. A haughty aristocrat has an excellent, plain gardener who tends his estate outside of Copenhagen. The master, however, never trusts the advice of the gardener or appreciates what he produces. He and his wife believe that the fruits and flowers grown by other gardeners are better, and when they constantly discover, to their chagrin, that their very own gardener's work is considered the best by the royal families, they hope he won't think too much of himself. Then, the storyteller Andersen comments (p. 1018):

> He didn't; but the fame was a spur, he wanted to be one of the best gardeners in the country. Every year he tried to improve some of the vegetables and fruits, and often he was successful.

It was not always appreciated. He would be told that the pears and apples were good but not as good as the ones last year. The melons were excellent but not quite up to the standard of the first ones he had grown.

The gardener must constantly prove himself, and one of his great achievements is his use of an area to plant "all the typical common plants of Denmark, gathered from forests and fields" (p. 1020), which flourish because of his nursing care and devotion. So, in the end, the owners of the castle must be proud of the gardener because the whole world beat the drums for his success. "But they weren't really proud of it. They felt that they were the owners and that they could dismiss Larsen if they wanted to. They didn't, for they were decent people, and there are lots of their kind, which is fortunate for the Larsens" (p. 1021).

In other words, Andersen himself had been fortunate, or at least this was the way he ironically viewed his career at the end of his life. Yet there is something pathetically sad about this story, given the fact that Andersen wrote it at the end of his life and continued to feel unappreciated in Denmark. The gardener Larsen is obviously the storyteller Andersen, and the garden with all its produce is the collection of fairy tales that he kept cultivating and improving throughout his life. The owners of the garden are Andersen's patrons and may be associated with the Collin family and other upper-class readers in Denmark. We must remember that it was generally known that the Collin family could never come to recognize Andersen as a *Digter* but thought of him as a fine popular writer. Andersen, whose vanity was immense and unquenchable, was extremely sensitive to criticism, and he petulantly and consistently complained that he felt undervalued in Denmark, while other European countries recognized his genius. Such treatment at home, despite the fact that he considered himself a most loyal servant, whether real or projected, became symbolized in this tale. The reference to the "common plants," which the gardener cultivates, pertains to the folk motifs and everyday objects he employed and enriched so they would bloom aesthetically on their own soil. Andersen boasts that he, the gardener, has made Denmark famous, for pictures are taken of this garden and circulated throughout the world. Yet, it is within the confines of servitude and patronage that the gardener works, and the dominated voice of the narrator, even though ironic, rationalizes the humiliating ways in which his masters treat Larsen: they are "decent" people. But, one must wonder — and the tension of the discourse compels us to do so — that, if the gardener is superb and brilliant, why doesn't he rebel and quit his job? Why does the gardener suffer such humiliation and domination? Why doesn't he emigrate?

Andersen pondered these questions often and presented them in many of his tales, but he rarely suggested alternatives or rebellion. Rather, he placed safety before idealism, choosing moral compromise over moral outrage and individual comfort and achievement over collective struggle and united goals. He aimed for identification with the power establishment that humiliates subjects rather than opposition to autocracy to put an end to exploitation through power. The defects in Andersen's ideological perspective are not enumerated here to insist that he should have learned to accept squalor and the disadvantages of poverty and struggle, or that he should have become a radical like Heinrich Heine and live in exile. They are important because they are the telling marks in the historical reception of his tales. Both the happy and sad endings of his narratives infer that there is an absolute or a divine, harmonious power, and that unity of an essentialist ego and salvation are possible under such power. Such a projection, however, was actually that of a frustrated and torn artist who was obliged to compensate for an existence that lacked harmonious proportions and autonomous power. Andersen's life was one based on servility, and his tales were endeavors to justify a false consciousness: literary exercises in the legitimation of a social order to which he subscribed.

Whether the discourse of such a dominated writer be a monologue with himself or a dialogue with an audience who partakes of his ideology, he still can never feel at peace with himself. It is thus the restlessness and the dissatisfaction of the dominated artist that imbue his work ultimately with the qualitative substance of what he seeks to relate. Ironically, the power of Andersen's fairy tales, for him and for his readers, has very little to do with the power he respected. It emanates from the missing gaps, the lapses, which are felt when the compromises are made under compulsion, for Andersen always painted happiness as adjusting to domination no matter how chosen one was. Clearly, then, Andersen's genius, despite his servility, rested on his inability to prevent himself from loathing all that he admired.

The Discourse of Rage and Revenge: Controlling Children

Children are fervent in their looking forward to things, whereas adults can lose a sense of what is there for the taking. The child, it seemed to Freud, was the virtuoso of desire, for whom the meaning of life could only be its satisfactions. And yet it was this appetite — the individual's lifeline — that seemed most under threat from within and from without: from the death instinct and from what Freud referred to rather abstractly as culture.

Adam Phillips, The Beast in the Nursery

It is not generally known in North America and the United Kingdom that Andersen's fairy tales were part of a major breakthrough in Danish children's literature, part of the rise of the Danish Golden Age in the nineteenth century that produced notable writers, poets, philosophers, and artists.[1] Before Andersen created his unusual tales, important pioneer writers began introducing folk tales and fairy tales to the Danish reading public. Adam Oehlenschläger translated fairy tales by German authors in *Eventyr af forskellige digtere* (*Fairy Tales by Various Authors*, 1816). Matthias Winther published *Danske Folkeventyr* (*Danish Folk Tales*, 1823), intended more for people interested in folklore than for children. About ten years later, Christian Molbech produced *Dansk bog I Prosa, til Brug ved Sprogundervisning I Modersmålet* (*Danish Prose for Language Teaching in the Mother Tongue*, 1832), which included six of the Grimms' tales. Most important for Andersen's development were Bernhard Severin Ingemann's *De underjordiske* (*Goblins*, 1817) and *Nye Eventyr og Fortællinger* (*Fairy Tales and Stories*, 1820). There were other imaginative works for children and Danish translations of fairy tales by the Brothers Grimm and the German romantics Ludwig Tieck, Joseph von Eichendorff, Adalbert von Chamisso, Friedrich de La Motte-Fouqué, and E. T. A. Hoffmann, whose works Andersen knew. As Finn Hauberg Mortsensen makes clear:

> These Golden Age efforts made children's culture visible and significant; prosperity made it possible; the new family structure made it necessary. But Andersen's discovery of childhood was more profound than that of other Danish Golden Age writers. In his fairy tales children's literature was elevated both aesthetically and psychologically to parity with literature for adults. Whereas the typical children's book throughout the rest of the century was marked by a cozy Biedermeier style, the Romanticism and the modernity in Andersen's texts brought them into dialogue with both the child and the adult, albeit on premises which were completely innocent.[2]

While it is somewhat true that Andersen "innocently" inscribed himself into children's literature, he did not realize how dangerous this inscription would be, for his "discovery" of childhood opened him up to more painful feelings of loss and rage than he realized: unfulfilled desires and needs came back to haunt him. To "save" himself he used the fairy-tale form to sublimate fomenting anxieties, disturbing desires, and furious rage: the fairy tale became his compensation for feelings of misrecognition and lack. Andersen wrote to understand himself and to make himself understood, and he employed the figures of children and childhood as tropes to speak out against the abuse he felt — often in sympathy with children and, at the same time, to put the child in his proper "Christian" place. In the process, he voiced fervent desires and disappointments that he sought to control and regulate. As we have seen in the previous chapter, this regulation frequently led to a discourse of the dominated, especially when he sought to rationalize his outrage at the injustices he felt. Yet, there were also "rebellious" stories, sweet tales of revenge that gave him deep pleasure and set standards of moral justification that were shared by many of his readers. These were mainly stories that introduced children as the major protagonists. It is through their voice that he exposed not only social contradictions, but also his own eccentric behavior and his need to control possible outbreaks that might reveal his inner secret life. Andersen was not as innocent as he seemed when he began writing fairy tales for children. He had his own design of morality and idealism that he rationalized as the intelligent design of God, and there is something perverse in his use of children to illustrate not only how proper behavior should work, but how sexuality should be governed. Andersen cleaned up sexuality, which he regarded as messy, and his cleansing process with children as objects needs greater exploration.

Strange to say, despite all posthumous recognition of Andersen as a brilliant writer for children, few critics have taken the time to investigate what it is that made Andersen such an appealing conventional writer for children and adults. To my knowledge, few scholars have investigated Andersen's concept of childhood, how children were conceived and con-figured in his tales, and how they represent a tension between "civilization and its discontents," to borrow a phrase from Freud, that forms and informs the dramatic conflict of many of his best tales — and some that receive very little attention. Since it would be difficult in a short chapter to analyze all the pertinent Andersen tales that use children and child-hood in significant ways, I want to focus on a select number of key texts[3] to explore how he tried to deal with his appetites to adjust to a world that denied him the fulfillment of pleasure, and I want to base my analysis in part on the work of the British child psychotherapist Adam Phillips.

Among the many books Phillips has written, *The Beast in the Nursery: On Curiosity and Other Appetites* is perhaps the most helpful for examin-ing why Andersen's reliance on children and childhood in his fairy tales became so significant for his (mal-)adjustment to a Danish upper-class society that continually frustrated his deepest desires. Phillips argues that our appetites (understood as interests in life) are what inspire us to enjoy life to the fullest. The difficulty for us as human beings is that we cannot always gratify our appetites the way we want, and we must learn to defer gratification — a key notion in Freud's *Civilization and Its Discontents*. As Phillips comments:

> Being realistic is a better guarantee of pleasure; it is an injunc-tion to want sensibly. The child may expect the earth of himself and others, but if he grows up properly, he will begin to want something else. But what happens to wanting when it isn't want-ing everything, and when it isn't wanting what one wants? Or, to put it another way — from an adult point of view, as it were — how do we decide what a good story about wanting is? And which stories will sustain our appetite, which is, by definition

our appetite for life? Even to want death you have to be alive. Morality is the way we set limits to wanting; the way we redescribe desiring so that it seems to work for us.[4]

We tend to view childhood as a singular phase in our lives, and once we have moved through it, childhood is left behind us for good. On the contrary, Phillips argues, our very early appetites that manifest themselves in childhood, such as curiosity about sex and relish for sensual experience, remain very much essential driving forces within us. However, the civilizing process, representative of the reality principle, insists on social regulation and compliance with norms of acceptable behavior and tends to dampen the appetites — it can even kill them unless we keep the conflict between our drives for pleasure and social restraints alive. It is through creative sublimation, learning how to articulate and satisfy our drive for pleasure, Phillips suggests, that we can learn to adapt to culture's demands, to become acculturated, while fulfilling distinct desires that enable our different personalities to flourish. Phillips cogently summarizes what maturation entails:

> Growing up then becomes the necessary flight from inarticulateness, from the less affectively organized self, a self without its best behaviors to be on, a self that suffers and enjoys at a pitch that the grown-ups often find daunting. In the old, modern fable of civilization and its discontents, either the child or the culture is demonized. But if we redescribe development as not simply the progressive acquisition of linguistic, and therefore moral, competence, we may be better able to nurture in children the necessary to-and-fro between the articulate selves; a to-and-fro that might be sustainable throughout life rather than having its last gasp during adolescence, or in mystical states, which are always subject to so much fascination and suspicion by those who ironize them (so-called perversion is always a compromised mysticism).[5]

It is not easy for most human beings, however, to accept the to-and-fro of everyday life, especially when the poles that mark the boundaries of this civilizing process freeze and become rigid, making us feel trapped, disappointed, and angry. If we want more than society can afford us materially or spiritually, if we become excessive in our demands for pleasure, we can easily become psychotic in our pursuit of the impossible and may cross the moral and ethical boundaries of society. If we are severely curtailed by the social codes, laws, and customs of a restrictive society that are unjust and oppressive, we feel enraged and humiliated and will try to seek revenge by trespassing the limits. Sometimes the disparities between what we want to be and what we actually think we are become so great that we explode and vent our anger in indiscriminate ways. In each case, rage plays an important role in determining our identities, and rage can be a just expression born out of discontent. Anger and rage reveal our morality and idealism. This is indeed the case with Andersen, and there is a key passage about "just rage" in Phillips's book that reveals a great deal about the inner workings of Andersen's psyche and how his stories may have "sprouted" from this justifiably enraged psyche:

> It is as though our morality, as disclosed by our anger, is a kind of private madness, a secret personal religion of cherished values that we only discover, if at all, when they are violated. The virtues we can consciously formulate and try to abide by are, one might say, our official morality. Our unofficial, more idiosyncratic morality is only available, so to speak, through humiliation. Once you know who or what humiliates you, you know what it is about yourself that you ultimately value, that you worship. Tell me what makes you enraged — what makes you feel truly diminished — and I will tell you what you believe or what you want to believe about yourself. What, that is, you imagine you need to protect to sustain your love of life.[6]

When we explode in anger and rage, we are not really in control of ourselves. The emotions we express are inarticulate. It is through the mode or genre of revenge, Phillips maintains, that we can gain redress. "If rage renders us helpless, revenge gives us something to do. It organizes our disarray. It is one way of making the world, or one's life, make sense. Revenge turns rupture into story."[7]

Rage is important for us because it connects us to our infancy when we are confronted with primal disillusion, that is, when we are forced to realize that we are not omnipotent, that all our wishes and needs cannot be obtained through our own power, and that we are dependent on other people. The dominant tendency in the institutions of "civilized" society fosters behavior and thinking that lead toward cooperation, compliance, or amnesia. Growing up can be a numbing process. We are disposed toward minimizing pain and conflict, rationalizing humiliation, and accepting the injustices of life. It is often through humiliation and rage that we recall the sensual pleasures of our body in childhood that indicated our instinctual love of life. Returning to childhood through literate articulation, therefore, does not necessarily mean a nostalgic longing for a primal state of innocence, but an endeavor to keep alive curiosity, imagination, interests, and a pursuit of sensual pleasure. It is an attempt to cling to lost idealism and morality. To write about and for children is not necessarily, as many critics have maintained, an act of abuse, concealment of sexuality, or manipulation of children, but it can also be an act of resistance. It is thus the figure of the outraged, enraged, and humiliated child who articulates an adult author's desire to engage society and to expose its contradictions. On the other hand, it is the punished, virtuous, and compromised child figure who articulates an adult author's desire to be accepted by society to which he delegates the right to judge and evaluate him. Either way, it is true, the author is manipulative, and the morality of the rage can easily turn to immoral acts against children and their appetites.

Andersen could go both ways as a writer and individual. He could be compliant and rebellious. He could be polite and outrageous. He was also apparently bisexual and did not know how to deal effectively with his bisexuality. Perhaps the only unifying force in his character was his discontentment and sense of just rage. It is discontentment with himself and society that drove him to become such a keen revengeful writer who set moral standards and ideal goals to which everyone should aspire. Though he often served as an apologist for the principles of domination in his narratives, he also acted out his feelings of rage that he sought to keep alive in provocative stories. At times he turned his rage against upper-class society and children, and other times he turned it against himself as though he loathed himself for not allowing his inner urges to be expressed. This tension between hatred of a superficial repressive society that constrained his urges and fear of his unfulfilled sexual desires, which he condemned as transgression, is at the basis of some of his most intriguing fairy tales in which he used children to test and play out his ideals and morals. In formulating rules of etiquette, behavior, and belief for his children figures, Andersen touched personal tensions closely wired to social tensions, and this touching may account for his wide appeal to young and adult readers, even today.

One of his earliest fairy tales, "The Naughty Boy" (1836), which is very rarely discussed, reads like a programmatic statement about how he would use child figures in his tales to try to tame the appetites and

The Naughty Boy (1893) illustrated by J. R. Weguelin in *The Little Mermaid and Other Stories*

curiosity. At the same time, this tale reflects how Eros, the child, resists arbitrary restraints and takes revenge on the world by piercing people's hearts. This very short allegorical tale is a clear illustration about how the unsettled Andersen sought to unsettle his readership, and about the elusiveness of art and children, both of which can penetrate our hearts when we least expect to be stirred. To control the uncontrollable through art was Andersen's goal, and it is the heart of this story.

The plot is seemingly simple: An old poet sits by a cozy fire on a stormy night. All of a sudden, he hears a knocking on the door and admits a little boy, stark naked, water streaming down his golden hair. The only things he carries with him are a bow and arrows. The boy, who resembles an angel, would have certainly died if the kind poet had not let him into the house. Once the boy is resuscitated, he begins to dance about the room in joy. The old poet remarks that the boy's bow and arrows are spoiled. However, Cupid picks up the bow and arrows and proves they are fine by shooting an arrow and piercing the old poet's heart. At this point the narrator informs us:

> The old poet lay on the floor, weeping. He had really been hit right in the heart. "Oh… oh…" he moaned. "The mischievous child! I am going to tell all the other boys and girls to beware of Cupid and never to play with him, so he cannot do them any harm."
>
> All the boys and girls who were warned by the old poet did their best to be on the alert against Cupid; but he fooled them anyway, because he is very cunning.[8]

Nobody can stop Cupid. He shoots his arrows at young and old everywhere — in schools, parks, and churches. Finally, the narrator comments tongue in cheek:

> Cupid is a rascal! Don't ever have anything to do with him! Imagine, he once shot your poor old grandmother, right through the heart; it's so long ago that it no longer hurts, but she hasn't forgotten it. Pooh! That mischievous Cupid! Now you know what he is like and what a naughty boy he is.[9]

On one level, the story is about the toppling of "old poetry," the old order, and the rise of the young spirit, left out in the dark. The insistent Cupid, banging on the door of a poet, apparently comfortable and content with himself, takes his revenge. He wants to inspire the old poet with love. But the poet, representing the old order, resists the power of love. He is too feeble, however, to stop the force of Eros. Love and imagination triumph. But it is through the backdoor, so to speak, that love and poetry enter the hearts and souls of people who are warned to be on their guard. Cupid is supposedly dangerous and uncontrollable, and can strike at any moment.

Andersen attaches great importance to the figure of the child as Cupid, who is a menace to society and yet is so necessary for the reproduction of the species and can never be forgotten. The irony of the narrative brings out what Andersen wanted and feared most: pursuit of his powerful appetites and enjoyment of his erotic drives. Andersen associates children with these appetites and drives, and throughout all his fairy tales and stories, he places them in situations in which they must learn restraint. To act upon one's desires without the guidance of God is a sin and must be punished. Cupid is indeed naughty and should not be followed. Love should be sacred and chaste. Above all, Andersen implied in most of his fairy tales that the child should not love himself or herself, that is, should not indulge its desires, but should instead conform to Andersen's ideal of the virtuous Christian child. Andersen is surprisingly rigid in the demands he places upon his child figures. He is compassionate when the children in his tales are downtrodden and turn to God for guidance. He is severe and punitive when they pursue their dreams that involve sensual and sexual exploration. Whoever places himself or herself in God's hands and acts according to Andersen's own ideal moral principles of proper Christian behavior will be rewarded. It is through God that they will also exact revenge. Whoever seeks carnal knowledge and wants to explore his or her own sensual desires is dangerous and must be controlled or punished.

Andersen's views of children and childhood were not static. They were conflicted because he was always subconsciously drawn to the "naughty boy," and this attraction bothered him. As I have proposed above, it is exactly this unresolved conflict that forms the dramatic tension of his tales throughout his life. His constant return to this conflict indicates how vital it was for him, and in each tale he wrote, he reelaborated the problematic of fulfilling sensual desires as a moral dilemma that was and remains a moral dilemma for his readers, even today. Andersen does not become more insightful or aware of himself in the course of writing his tales: he did not come to any greater enlightenment about himself toward the end of the life. He simply became more proficient in using the genre of the fairy tale and fantastic story to express his anger against the world and take revenge through storytelling. He employed child figures to fend off erotic proclivities and create ideal possibilities that revealed both his own and society's contradictions. In the process, he left behind him tantalizing tales that need to be examined with great care for what they say about children and how they use children.

In contrast to "naughty Cupid," there are generally two models of comportment and decorum that he registers in his tales: the good girl, who is mainly self-sacrificial, and the good boy, whose zeal, innocence, and talents lead him to fame and fortune. Andersen weaves or configures these models laden with Christian symbols, if you will, throughout his tales, and they tend to be very gender specific. Given his unconscious misogynist attitudes toward women, he was bound to make distinctions between the proper roles and identities that girls and boys were to assume, as did most people in Danish society of his time — not to mention most Europeans and Americans. His girl figures are most fascinating because he clearly identified with many of them, and the punishments and tortures he created or invented for them were indications of the shame that he felt about himself, his ambivalent rage against society, and the ideal behavior that he sought to construct through the metaphorical destiny of his "heroine." Let us examine a few stories, beginning with "The Red Shoes," which is among his most well-known and most egregious in its brutal treatment of children, especially girls.

To be fair to Andersen, his horrific punishments of his "naughty" child figures were not unusual for his time. Charles Dickens' works are filled with examples of how children were abused in the nineteenth century, but he generally sympathized with the children and placed the blame for their sins on adult society. On the other hand, as I have already mentioned, Heinrich Hoffmann in *Struwwelpeter* (1845), the most famous picture book for children in the nineteenth century, delights in the mutilation of children who are deemed sinners, and the Brothers Grimm also provided horrifying examples of children who, for example, deserved such cruel treatment as being turned into logs because of their disobedience. What makes Andersen's fairy tales slightly different are his constant sanctimonious references to Christian strictures and the ferocity of the punishments he doled out to his child figures, especially girls. There is an implosion of rage in "The Red Shoes," written in 1846, that is highly disturbing.

Instead of taking revenge on society or the oppressors that restricted his movements, Andersen channels his rage in this story against his own creative spirit, against Eros, against curiosity represented by a girl, so that the explosion of his anger becomes an implosion that actually subdues a lively spirit and causes the death of instinctual curiosity. In the course of his story, he disseminates notions of childhood that call for the incarceration of the appetites and conformity to the religious penal rules of his times. Karen, his innocent victim, is selected as his exemplary figure/ victim to demonstrate proper moral behavior and decorum in times of crisis. A poor village girl, she is adopted by a rich lady when her mother dies, and she is forced to abandon red shoes, which she thinks are her good luck charm that attracted the attention of the rich lady. Later, when she sees a princess dressed in a white dress and red Moroccan leather shoes, she finds them the most desirable things in the world. She deceives her foster mother and convinces her to purchase similar red shoes for her confirmation, and she even wears them to communion, despite the fact that the old lady scolds her and that they cause her to lose control of herself. She is clearly obsessed by the red shoes; they have become her fetish. When her foster mother becomes deathly ill, Karen decides to go to a ball rather than to tend the old woman. However, once she puts on the red shoes, they carry her away from the ball over fields and meadows and through the graveyard until she reaches the church door, barred by a stern angel with a shining sword (p. 292):

> "You shall dance," he said, "dance in your red shoes until you become pale and thin. Dance till the skin on your face turns yellow and clings to your bones as if you were a skeleton. Dance you shall from door to door, and when you pass a house where proud and vain children live, there you shall knock on the door so that they will see you and fear your fate. Dance, you shall dance.... Dance!"

And dance she does, poor Karen, for days and weeks until she comes to the executioner's cottage. She begs him to cut off her feet, which he does, and then he makes wooden feet for her. Afterward, she learns the psalm that a penitent sings and goes to live with the minister. Totally devoted to God, humble and pious, Karen joins the congregation and receives God's mercy so that "the sunshine filled Karen's heart till it so swelled with peace and happiness that it broke. Her soul flew on a sunbeam up to God; and up there no one asked her about the red shoes" (p. 294).

If total abnegation of one's self, desires, and appetites will bring about happiness, then we can imagine Karen happy in God's paradise. But what if we think children's curiosity should be encouraged and cultivated? What if we believe that we must try to keep our own childlike curiosity alive to enjoy life to its fullest? It is really not difficult to interpret the symbol of the red shoes that cause eternal movement. For Andersen, it was clearly a sign of sin, not unlike the little red riding hood or the scarlet letter, but the sign of sin is also a sign of curiosity and desire that Andersen wanted to repress and suppress. And it is from a struggle within himself that he conceives a model of the good girl: clean, often in white clothes, self-denying, obedient, respectful, shameful, industrious, devoutly religious, and God-fearing. In her upbringing, there is not one hint of pleasure. Andersen's story outlines a childhood of dread, a childhood in which the girl is to learn to dread her own desires and impulses. If naughty Cupid could not be caught in one of his first stories, Andersen made sure that the tantalizing figure of erotic desire would be caught and punished in later stories, at least, those that were apparently addressed to children and parents looking for tips on how to raise children. We can see other dread-ful examples in such tales as "The Little Mermaid," whose voice is taken away from her and her movement curtailed, or "The Girl Who Stepped on Bread," in which a proud and arrogant girl is punished by being sent to hell for discarding some bread in order to keep her shoes clean.

There is, of course, a more positive away to analyze Andersen's tale and to view it as a critique of the socioreligious code that drives a young girl to destroy herself. In her highly insightful essay, "Red Shoes and Bloody Stumps,"[10] Erin Mackie explains how significant the red shoes can be as fetish if one acknowledges the deep powers of the fetish and gets in touch with it:

> But really getting in touch with the fetish involves not the posi-tivist assignation of value — critical, social, and political — to concepts outside the fetish's logic, but the recognition of the critical, even revolutionary powers of the fetish itself. Indeed, one way to talk about positivism lies in the identification of those notions it fixes against the (false) fetishized values it critiques.... Fetish is pitted against fetish in an interdependent logic where each is "contaminated" with the talismanic trace of the other it would displace. In Andersen's tale the red shoes become fetishes of Karen's misplaced values, the shoes operating as a counter-fetish to reveal and transgress what, from the perspective of an underclass, beautiful, and ambitious young girl, is the bad juju of a socioreligious system fixed against her.[11]

The red shoes are thus similar to the figure of the recurring figure of Cupid in "The Naughty Child": they are magical like our appetites, for they cannot be tamed on this earth, and Karen's obsessive appetite reveals the injustices and mortifying humiliation that any child from the lower classes must suffer for desiring to improve his or her lot. Though she is punished for her fetish, the harsh punishment does not fit the crime, and one must wonder why a girl's innocent longing for some beauty in her life is considered a sin. The ending of Andersen's tale is, as Mackie points out, clearly contrived and relies on a deus ex machina in the person of the angel. Andersen sought unsuccessfully to cap his own curiosity, attraction, and appetites aroused in his childhood by bottling them. Afraid of where they might lead him and did lead him, he enacted a kind of self-punishment on the poor girls in his tales for their transgressions and rewarded their submission to a religious code that never led to self-fulfillment.

Andersen only treated girls leniently if they were humble and devout. In "The Little Match Girl," a forlorn soul is afraid to return home because she had not sold any matches and her father might beat her. As she lights the matches in an alley to keep herself warm, she has lovely visions of a pleasant home life. Though these visions do not prevent her death, they do enable the reader to see how she is rewarded for her simple piety by her grandmother, who fetches her and takes her to God. In "What the Whole Family Said," little Maria celebrates her birthday by asserting how lovely it is to live, and her godfather supports this view by stating that "life was the best of all fairy tales" (p. 999). It is not clear at first what Andersen means in this little vignette, but it soon becomes evident when the godfather instructs Maria that everything that has happened or will happen was written down in the Bible. Furthermore, he adds, "the older you get the clearer you see that God is with you — both in adversity and when Fortune shines upon you — and that life is the very best fairy tale, and it is He who has given it to us for all eternity" (p. 1001).

The good girl is the pious child who will always be saved by God as long as she has faith in his omnipotence. There is hardly a girl or woman in Andersen's fairy tales who triumphs in life because she is adventurous and daring — with the possible exception of Gerda in "The Snow Queen." Even the shepherdess in "The Shepherdess and the Chimney Sweep" loses her courage in her flight from a forced marriage when she encounters the vast wide world. She returns to the parlor ready to sacrifice herself and submit to the rule of the Chinese mandarin. What is most interesting about the girl figures in Andersen's tales is that they often die and are transformed into spirits serving God. They rarely are allowed to develop, and if they do, their "realms of happiness" are associated with domesticity. A girl is to be domesticated, to become a domestic if not on earth, then in God's paradise.

The Little Match Girl (1887) illustrated by Joseph J. Mora in *Hans Andersen's Fairy Tales*

It is much different with Andersen's male figures, whose tales are more often than not stories about the rise from rags to riches and fame. As is well known, Andersen was very familiar with Adam Oehlenschläger's play *Aladdin* or *The Wonderful Lamp* (1805), and one motif in his tales about boys involves the opportunism that they must embrace to survive in a class-ridden society, and the other is the decency, kindness, and trust in God that they must demonstrate to achieve what they are apparently born to achieve. In both cases, Andersen channels his rage outward in explosive ways. The fairy tale becomes his genre of just revenge.

The most obvious example of his opportunistic and somewhat violent young hero is the soldier in "The Tinderbox." Though he is not a boy, he is obviously very young, and as a child figure, he represents for young readers the desire for omnipotence at all costs that drives them and that they miraculously achieve. It is also clear that this young soldier has been storing a certain rage for some time. Why else does he explode and chop off the witch's head at the slightest provocation? The story is well known and quick to review. The soldier helps a witch by fetching a tinderbox from beneath the ground. He is rewarded with gold but wants to know why the tinderbox is so important. The witch refuses to tell him, and so he kills her. Then he takes the tinderbox into town and discovers its magic secret: if he strikes the tinderbox, a dog with eyes as big as teacups appears and grants him any wish he makes. So he wishes for riches and also nocturnal visits with the princess. But he is discovered by the king and queen, and they have him thrown in jail (without the tinderbox) to be hanged. Right before he is to be executed, he is granted one last wish, and he asks to smoke a pipe of tobacco. He takes out his tinderbox, which he had recovered thanks to a boy, and strikes it three times. Three dogs appear, and they attack the judge and royal council and send the king and queen flying, never to be seen again. The soldier marries the princess, and they become the new king and queen.

This is one of the few tales Andersen wrote that has no apparent moral, unless one understands that the soldier has already been mistreated in the war and has been a puppet of the king. If one assumes this mistreatment, common in related folk tales, the only morality is one based on just rage: the lower-class hero takes revenge on the upper classes. He shows no mercy because he has obviously been badly treated by his superiors, and he proves that he knows how to survive in a dog-eat-dog world. What is significant here in the portrayal of the young, Aladdin-type hero is that he is smart, ruthless, opportunistic, and decisive. The boy adventurer makes his mark in the world, and he deserves to be recognized because of his talents. Such desire for omnipotence is an infantile urge that can never be fully satisfied, and as Andersen well knew, the pursuit of omnipotence could drive a person crazy or make a man into a criminal. Therefore, he was hesitant to preach this message to young boys and often tempered his rage according to his own personal Christian code. Instead of the rebel, he often chose to portray the "good boy" in his tales.

Generally speaking, the good boy, like the good girl, must demonstrate absolute faith in God, as was demonstrated in one of Andersen's earliest fairy tales, "The Traveling Companion," which I have already discussed at some length. Another example, also based on the folk tradition, is "Little Tuck," about a boy who is babysitting his little sister Gustava while doing his homework; he is supposed to memorize all the towns and cities of Zealand for his geography lesson. When his mother returns home, she peeks out the window and sees an old washerwoman who is laboriously carrying water from the pump in the square. She asks Tuck to help, and he graciously complies. When he returns home, it is late at night, and he goes to bed without finishing his homework assignment. As he dozes off with the geography book beneath his pillow to try to soak in the lessons through osmosis, he feels the washerwoman kissing him and saying to him, "It would be a sin and a shame … if you did not know your lesson tomorrow in school because you helped me. Now I shall help you and the Lord will help us both" (p. 331). Indeed, he goes on marvelous adventures in his dreams and visits the towns and cities of Zealand, learning about their history, and he also has a bright future predicted for him. The next morning he jumps out of bed, and the washerwoman comes by, thanks him for his help, and wishes that all his dreams will come true. Andersen ends with a typical wry comment: "Little Tuck didn't remember what he had dreamed; but Our Lord did" (p. 333).

Andersen based the plot of his tale on a simple folk-tale type in which a poor old woman (either a fairy or witch) appears at a well in need of water. She asks for help, generally from a good peasant maiden, and in turn for the help, the maiden returns home and pearls and diamonds come pouring from her mouth when she speaks to her stepmother, while jewels are combed from her hair. Then her stepmother sends her ugly daughter to the well to reap the same reward, except that this daughter maltreats the old woman and is punished. There are hundreds of variants of this tale, and many involve a young boy who sometimes throws a rock at an old woman carrying water or oil. Andersen's charming simple version is a didactic tale that depicts the benefits of generosity, kindness, and hard work. Throughout his tales, there are boys like little Tuck, whose determination, goodness, and innocence are recognized and blessed by God, and they are rewarded. Such tales did not emanate directly from Andersen's rage, but they did reinforce the Aladdin "revenge" motif that runs throughout many of his tales about young protagonists, who, with the help of God or magical powers, rise against all expectations to become rich and famous.

The Bronze Pig (1887) illustrated by Joseph J. Mora in *Hans Andersen's Fairy Tales*

"The Bronze Pig" is another good example. It is a more complicated tale than "Little Tuck" and is set in Florence at the early part of the nineteenth century. A poor beggar boy, unable to earn any money, falls asleep on the back of a water fountain made in the shape of a pig. Late that night the pig becomes alive and carries the boy through the city to the gallery in the arcade of the Palazzo degli Uffizi. There he is able to see the marvelous marble statues and paintings for the first time in his life. As the boy gazes at the Medici Venus, the narrator comments, "on either side of her stood a marble statue, each proving that man's spirit and art can give life, can create it from lifeless stone. One of the figures was of a man grinding his sword; the other showed two gladiators wrestling: for beauty's sake the weapon was sharpened and the men fought" (p. 158). The boy is also struck by the painting of Agnolo Bronzino's *Jesus Descending into the Underworld* because of the innocent children waiting for Christ to lead them to paradise. After the boy and the pig view the paintings and leave the arcade, the pig says, "Thank yourself and God bless you!... I have helped you and you have helped me, for only when an innocent child sits on my back, do I become alive and have the strength to run as I have tonight. Yes, I even let the light from the lamp beneath the Blessed Virgin shine upon me" (p. 159).

They continue on their way to the Church of Santa Croce, where the boy is once again inspired by the art works in the church. The next morning he awakes on top of the bronze pig and realizes that he must return to his mother, who is expecting money from him. When the beggar boy shows up, his mother beats him, but he escapes and takes refuge in the Church of Santa Croce. Fortunately for him, a kind glove maker takes pity on him and brings him to his home. After speaking to the beggar boy's mother, the glove maker and his wife decide to keep the boy as an apprentice. When the boy is asked to help a painter, a neighbor, carry his paints to the Uffizi, he recognizes the paintings and marble statues and feels the urge to become a painter. Some time later the boy is blamed unfairly by the glove-maker's wife for losing her little dog, and the painter makes peace among them and gives the boy some drawings as a gift. "If you can draw," the child thinks, "then you can call the world your own" (p. 164). So he begins to teach himself how to draw. Once again he has an altercation with the glove-maker's wife because he had tied the dog to make it sit still as a model. This time he is kicked out of the house, and the famous painter takes him under his wing. We learn that, years later, the young boy became a great artist but died shortly before his work was exhibited at the Academy of Art.

There are many themes in this undeservedly neglected tale, such as the power of art and the trials and tribulations of poverty. Clearly, Andersen wants to record the salvation of an innocent child through art, especially religious art. Furthermore, he does not shy away from depicting the impoverished conditions and abuse that poor children suffered during this time. However, in contrast to the destiny that he painted for little girls, this tale shows childhood as a test that the boy can pass. As in "Little

Tuck," the beggar boy is saved by inspiration and determination. Nor does he have to kill anyone to gain revenge, for he instinctively becomes aware that he can make his enraged feelings beautiful, that they can serve his art, a lesson that Andersen himself had been quick to learn. The beggar boy shapes the world around him instead of allowing the world to shape him or to deform him. It is clearly this indomitable spirit in the young boys and girls that Andersen wanted to flesh out in his tales. However, it was a zest for life that had to be controlled, refined, and sanctified. If left to their own devices, children might be overcome by their feelings; they could become tarnished or be seduced by evil forces. For instance, "The Snow Queen, a Fairy Tale Told in Seven Stories" reveals Andersen's strong belief that children cannot survive without faith in divine powers, and in order to save themselves, they must abandon themselves to the will of God. Many of Andersen's tales have Christian imagery and references that have been eliminated in twentieth-century editions, or simply neglected. We tend to forget that many of his tales are morality plays, especially those explicitly concerned with children. This is most clear in "Ib and Little Christina" and "The Snow Queen."

To a certain extent, "Ib and Little Christina" is a sentimental preview of "The Snow Queen," and it repeats Andersen's favorite story of chaste love, one that he never tired of telling: a boy and girl are drawn to each other in their youths, and promise each other that they will always love one another; however, they are separated. The girl appears to have more fortune than the boy, and when she is older, she marries someone else. The boy remains at home, leading a simple life and is saddened by his sweetheart's marriage. Then the tables turn: the young woman, associated with city life, falls in fortune and dies, and the young man, associated with the country, has a stroke of good luck and arrives in the city to fetch his former sweetheart only to find her dead. In "Ib and Little Christina," Ib remains devoted to Christina until her death in Copenhagen. Then he takes her daughter back to the country to raise her in nature.

Andersen varied this plot in different tales, but the overall message concerns Christian charity, humility and self-sacrifice. This is apparent when Ib and Christina, lost in the woods as youngsters, meet a gypsy woman. She offers them "wishing nuts," and Christina takes two of the nuts that contain a golden carriage with golden horses and ten necklaces, dresses, stockings, and hats. But Ib is left with a little black one. From this point on, their paths will diverge because it is obvious that Christina, like the little mermaid and like Karen in "The Red Shoes," values material things over the genuine country life and the deep love that Ib feels for her. She is more than happy to leave him and go to Copenhagen, where she lives in the lap of luxury. On the other hand, Ib stays in the country, and he makes his fortune because he finds a valuable relic while plowing his fields. He never overreaches. He digs into the fertile soil that provides all he needs. He even gains a measure of revenge thanks to his holding to moral principles: Christina dies impoverished, and the innocent Ib will raise her daughter named Christina. He will be in charge of her upbringing, and one can be guaranteed that he will not allow her to be attracted to luxury and the city. Andersen has a completely repressed and narrowly sentimental view of life: anyone who veers off the path of chaste love and indulges in sensuality will be punished or be hauled back on the clean right path. Boys and girls must learn to have faith, live simply, and place their destiny in the hands of the Lord.

This is the lesson to be learned in "The Snow Queen," which begins with a brilliant and humorous prologue-tale that explains how evil came to the world and why little Kai is kidnapped and placed at the mercy of evil forces. The narrator tells the reader that the most evil troll in the world had once invented a huge mirror that had the power of making anything good or beautiful seem horrid in its reflection, and anything evil and worthless to appear good and worthy. The trolls decide to carry the mirror to heaven to mock God and the angels, but on the way they drop the gigantic mirror so that it shatters into millions and billions of pieces. The result is that when any one of the splinters enters a person's eyes, he would see only the flaws of the world and the faults of the people. If a splinter enters a person's heart, the heart turns to ice. All this, of course, pleases the devil.

After this prologue, the narrator introduces us to the playmates Kai and Gerda, who are about ten years old. They listen to stories by an old grandmother, who tells them about the Snow Queen, who can turn hearts to ice, and that night Kai believes that he has seen the Snow Queen outside his window. During the summer, Kai and Gerda play together in a rose garden, and they sing a song that will become a refrain throughout the tale: "In the valley where the roses be / There the child Jesus you will see" (p. 237).

Soon thereafter two splinters strike Kai in his eye and heart, and his behavior begins to change. He becomes nasty and stops playing with Gerda. That winter, he is kidnapped by the Snow Queen, who carries him off to her realm in the North. The following spring Gerda decides

The Snow Queen (1887) illustrated by Joseph J. Mora in *Hans Andersen's Fairy Tales*

to go in pursuit of Kai, and her story of travails is well known. At first she is delayed by a good witch in her flower garden. Once she leaves this place, she is helped by a crow, a prince, and a princess and given a coach to travel to the Snow Queen's palace. However, the coach is attacked by ruthless robbers who kill everyone except Gerda. Fortunately, a robber girl takes a liking to her and gives Gerda a reindeer, mittens, and boots to continue on her quest to save Kai. After a Lapp woman aids her, Gerda goes to the Finnish woman near the Snow Queen's palace, and the reindeer expects her to give Gerda magic powers. But the Finnish woman explains to him (p. 257):

> I can't give her any more power than she already has! Don't you understand how great it is? Don't you see how men and animals must serve her; how else could she have come so far, walking on her bare feet? But she must never learn of her power; it is in her heart, for she is a sweet and innocent child. If she herself cannot get into the Snow Queen's palace and free Kai from the glass splinters in his heart, how can we help her?"

So the reindeer carries Gerda to the Snow Queen's garden and leaves her. When Gerda says her prayers, "a whole legion of little angels stood around her. They threw their spears at the snow monsters, and they splintered into hundreds of pieces. Little Gerda walked on unafraid, and the angels caressed her little feet and hands so she did not feel the cold" (p. 258). Once she finds Kai and weeps on his breast, her tears melt the ice and glass splinters in him, and she sings their psalm:

> Our roses bloom and fade away,
> Our infant Lord abides always.
> May we be blessed his face to see
> And ever little children be (p. 260).

Released from the spell of the Snow Queen, Kai rejoices, and together with Gerda they travel back to their city. As soon as they step through the doorway of the Grandmother's apartment, however, they realize that they have grown up. The Grandmother is sitting in the sunshine and reading aloud from her Bible: "Whosoever shall not receive the Kingdom of Heaven as a little child shall not enter therein" (p. 262). Gerda and Kai now understand the meaning of the psalm and sit and bask in the warmth of the summer day.

It would be interesting to compare this fairy tale to the German romantic Novalis's tale of "Roseblossom and Hyacinth," which Andersen may have known.[12] In Novalis's tale, Hyacinth is in perfect harmony with nature and Roseblossom, and when a strange man arrives and disturbs the boy's mind with a book (Reason), Hyacinth throws the book into a fire and departs on a mysterious quest. However, this quest turns out to be an existential one, and he finally arrives at the sacred dwelling of Isis. There he unveils the Egyptian goddess, only to find Roseblossom and reunite with her in eternal love. Implicit in Hyacinth's quest is that he must leave himself to find himself and the meaning of love. In the draft of another version of this tale, Hyacinth lifts the veil of Hyacinth only to find himself.

Novalis was concerned with the ontological quest of his protagonist, who is originally in touch with his feelings but suffers a breakdown when introduced to book learning. To recuperate the initial bliss he felt, he must follow his intuition and experience different environments before he is mature enough to face the truth of Isis. His growth is dependent on overcoming reason and combining his experience with a grasp of nature to uncover what he really desires in life. Novalis's tale is a recuperation of desire that forms the basis of adult action. Andersen's tale moralizes and tames desire.

"The Snow Queen" ends simply with the triumph of good over evil, and it depicts the child protagonists as adults who remain children at heart and devoted to a Christian stricture. In many ways, the tale is a baptismal ritual: Gerda and Kai must prove that they have expunged the evil in their bodies before they will be accepted in the kingdom of God. All children must prove their "innocence" if they want to be saved. Gerda is, of course, innocence incarnate, and she is one of the few female figures in Andersen's works who does not become contaminated. Moreover, she is much more active than most, perhaps because she is protected by angels. Andersen imagines that children can be infected by evil forces associated with a real devil, who holds them in his power. He also associates evil with cold reason that opposes basic good instincts. The Snow Queen's palace is on the "lake of the Mirror of Reason," and Kai is playing the "Game of Reason" when Gerda finds him. He can only learn to spell "eternity" after Gerda arrives and frees his heart. It is faith that children must learn to trust, and not reason, and it is blind trust in Christian faith that Andersen relentlessly preached in most of his fairy tales for children and adults. To be sure, his Christian faith was mystical and mixed with Ørsted's notions of divine intelligence.

As W. Glyn Jones has made clear,[13] Andersen believed in God and was a Lutheran, but he was not orthodox and never fully outlined his beliefs in his essays, diaries, or autobiographies. Nevertheless, when it came to the depiction of children and childhood in his fairy tales, it is apparent that the only good child is the Christian child, who serves God above all, and that God will punish or reward children if they keep the faith. The bond with God is somewhat mystical in the tales, although it is clear — in contrast to most folk tales and fairy tales before Andersen's time, which are secular and place fairies as the most omnipotent creatures — that the child must obey gender-specific, Christian principles of behavior to be accepted in God's paradise. What saves Andersen's tales from becoming Christian stories dripping with moral sentiments is his "innocent" depiction of the tension between the imaginative curiosity and appetites of his protagonists and the divine postulate calling upon them to submit to higher powers — and also to curb the rage that penetrates Andersen's tales.

Yet, one must also ask whether Andersen is really innocent. Was he really so guileless in how he arranged his child figures to exhibit behavior that called for reward and punishment? Do the morality and idealism of his rage excuse his manipulation of childhood and children figures? Does his innocence show his guilt? Did Andersen pander to adult conceptions of what children should be and how they should behave?

Andersen is not unlike another great writer of fantasy, namely J. M. Barrie of Peter Pan fame. Petulant, moody, disturbed, Barrie also catered to conventional notions of sexuality and childhood held by adults when he wrote about children. Moreover, there was a way in which Barrie used his fiction to conceal his desire for children and manipulate them for his own pleasure. In her controversial but convincing study *The Case of Peter Pan or The Impossibility of Children's Literature*, Jacqueline Rose explains how desire functions in Barrie's writings:

> Suppose, therefore, that what is at stake in Peter Pan is the adult's desire for the child. I am not using "desire" here in the sense of an act which is sought after or which must actually take place. It is not relevant, therefore, to insist that nothing ever happened, or that Barrie was innocent of any interest in sex (a point which is often made). I am using desire to refer to a form of investment by the adult in the child, and to the demand made by the adult on the child as the effect of that investment, a demand which fixes the child and then holds it in place. A turning to the child, or a circulating around the child — what is at stake here is not so much something which could be enacted as something which cannot be spoken.[14]

Though it would be unfair to both Barrie and Andersen to equate their techniques of writing and their unconscious motives behind their imaginings, there is something very similar in the fabric of their works that is disturbing. It is what Rose calls a sexual act "in which the child is used (and abused) to represent the whole problem of what sexuality is, or can be, and to hold that problem at bay."[15] In Andersen's fairy tales and stories, it is clear from the beginning in a tale like "The Naughty Boy" that Andersen does not know what to do with the child's appetites and his/her sexuality (polymorphous, perverse, bisexual) and thus tries to fix it and gender it in absolute terms in his writings. Andersen operated with and on all his child figures to ward off his anxieties about sex and to channel his rage. Yet by operating with principles of intelligent divine design to project how children and adults could protect their innocence (or recuperate innocence) under God's watchful eyes, Andersen sought to repress sexuality linked to the appetites, curiosity, and invention. His mode of revenge writing was chaste, and it involved not only his child figures. He also implicated all the adult figures and himself in weaving what he convinced himself was the Lord's design. Andersen was not an innocent writer. He is inculpated in his very own designs that fostered a myth of how an innocent, talented poor boy could, by God's grace, reach heavenly heights. Such a perverse myth circulates in many forms in our contemporary world and minimizes the diverse nature of human beings and the complex nature of identity formation. For Andersen, there was a formula, and if children veered from it and revealed they were not as innocent as they appeared, they would receive their just punishment and be mutilated, tortured, or put to death. Andersen, the so-called writer for children, could not tolerate the way children are in reality. What is saddest of all, however, is that he could not tolerate the child in himself.

The Cinematic Appropriation of Andersen's Heritage: Trivialization and Innovation

I'm Hans Christian Andersen, I've many a tale to tell.
And though I'm a cobbler, I'd say I tell them rather well.
I'll mend your shoes and I'll fix your boots when I have a
  moment free,
When I'm not otherwise occupied as a purple duck, or a mountain
  side, or a quarter after three.
I'm Hans Christian Andersen, that's me!

From the Samuel Goldwyn production, Hans Christian Andersen (1952)
Song composed by Frank Loesser and sung by Danny Kaye

For many people, young and old, who have grown up viewing the classic RKO film *Hans Christian Andersen*, produced in 1954 and starring the inimitable Danny Kaye, it is difficult to know who Hans Christian Andersen actually is and what really is significant about his tales. Like Andersen's own autobiography, *The Fairy Tale of My Life*, which he wrote to conceal many uncomfortable facets of his life, there is very little truth in this charming film, which distorts not only his life but also the meaning of many of the tales. Yet the powerful impact of *Hans Christian Andersen* is such that people continue to believe Andersen was a happy-go-lucky cobbler, unlucky in love, who sought to entertain children with his delightful storytelling. The problem with this rosy image of a highly neurotic man, who was afraid to love and had only occasional contact with children, is that it belies the profound and disturbing contribution that Andersen made to the fairy-tale tradition throughout the world.

103

But it is not just the 1954 cinematic version of Andersen's life that minimizes and trivializes Andersen's significance as a fairy-tale writer; it is also such films as *The Little Mermaid*, produced by the Walt Disney corporation in 1989. This film marked the resurgence of the Disney studio in the field of animated fairy-tale films while unfortunately simplifying the complex meaning of Andersen's fairy tale. Yet it is not only the Disney corporation that has appropriated and transformed the meaning of Andersen's tales to serve its own interests. There are many other directors and film studios that have used or exploited Andersen's tales so that their "original" meanings become corrupted and obfuscated. Some have even improved upon the original tales or developed themes in extraordinary ways that open new vistas on the contradictory aspects of Andersen's stories.

In the twentieth and twentieth-first centuries, the film adaptations of the classical tales by Andersen as well as those by the Brothers Grimm and Charles Perrault have become better known than the classical texts, which, in comparison, have virtually lost their meanings due to the fact that the films have replaced them. But comparison of the film adaptations with the original classical texts can be hazardous. For instance, we cannot fix the "original" significance of an Andersen fairy tale. In fact, we cannot determine the "authentic" meaning of any fairy tale. Nor do we know anything about Andersen's "true" intentions. At best, we can only study the structure, linguistic usage, prevalent themes, tendentious meanings, and ideology of Andersen's tales in a sociohistorical context to understand how they formed dispositions toward a reception, and how that reception reveals the attitudes and tastes of reading audiences during his time and in other sociohistorical contexts. It is, however, significant that Andersen's tales were more or less canonized while he was still alive, and this canonization also set the grounds for tendentious readings, that is, it predisposed readers to a consensual reception that has continued throughout the twentieth century and into the twenty-first.

Andersen did his best to control the reception of his tales. Vain as he was, he wanted history to remember him as a serious artist, a genius who created tales that adults would ponder and read in awe because of their profound meanings. He never intended for history to record his fame primarily as a writer of fairy tales for children. He would probably be disappointed and astounded to see what Hollywood and Disney have made out of his life and tales. On the other hand, he would probably be more intrigued by the European cinematic interpretations that probe his tales with greater imagination.

Nevertheless, fairy-tale films based on Andersen's texts cannot be judged by speculation of what he might have thought or on how closely or loosely the films are based on the printed word. As artistic works in their own right, the films demand to be appreciated and understood as representations that reflect upon Andersen's works but reflect primarily upon attitudes, tastes, customs, and tendencies in our own times. As part of the oral and literary genre of fairy tales that can be traced back to the sixteenth century, the films are an extension of this genre and a continuation of a multidimensional discourse that has framed very specific topics, such as intelligent design, the persecution of women, social prejudice, the nature of art, the abuse of children, miraculous transformation, and so on. For centuries people have employed imaginative projections and metaphorical language in narrative form to communicate their feelings and judgments about these topics, and they have repeated these tales with recognizable motifs and within recognizable contours that facilitate understanding. The fairy-tale films use the artistic and technical means of cinema to continue discussion about issues raised by the oral and literary fairy tales, but in new terms.

Fairy-tale films based on Andersen's tales add a new dimension to his stories and inadvertently comment on his role as a writer and on the function of fairy tales in the period from 1945 to the present. Their point of departure is always a reading of an Andersen text, at the very least, or a familiarity with the text, which is then appropriated as the basis for a film. The point of departure is also a parting of the ways, a taking apart of the text, breaking it down to re-form and reshape it through a medium that will amplify its meaning in many ways: a new script based on the ideas of the screenplay writer; actual images of the setting, clothes, and articles in the story invented and designed by many hands; full-fledged personalities of the characters portrayed by actors with unique talents; perspectives on the action determined by the camera angle and vision of the film's director; color and music that provide atmosphere; animated drawings created by numerous artists who design the characters and settings; voice-overs by actors whose abilities to speak in particular ways enliven apparently unreal characters. A fairy-tale film based on an Andersen fairy tale is never solely concerned with the Andersen text except as a point of departure to explore new cultural meanings and technical inventions, to experiment with aesthetical design, and to provide entertainment for a mass audience.

There are questions that we must ask, however, about the point of departure. For instance, why did the director and producer choose an Andersen fairy tale for the basis of their film? How seriously did they and their crews examine and interpret Andersen's work? That is, were they using his name and fame to promote their film as a commodity to make money? Did they intend to explore and elaborate on Andersen's text to shed new light on its meaning? Did they intend to add something new to our cultural knowledge of Andersen and his fairy tales, and did they succeed? Did they reduce Andersen's fairy tale to an appropriately self-censored film for children that infantilizes children? Whether these be live-action productions or animated films, how do they contribute to the general development of the fairy-tale film?

These are all important questions because Andersen's cultural heritage is being determined, especially in America, more by the cinematic adaptations and interpretations of his tales than by his texts or collections of his tales. This is not to argue that his tales are not being read today, but it is a fact that people, young and old, are reading less and less, and even their reading will be influenced by movies and TV. If Andersen is studied at all, it is in our universities, and even there, he has not been as widely examined as Perrault, the Grimms, and other fairy-tale writers. Nevertheless, there appears to be a struggle over his heritage and the meaning of his tales through cinematic adaptation. On the one side, there is the American viewpoint that tends toward a commodification and trivialization of his tales; on the other side, the Europeans, especially in Russia, France, Czechoslovakia, and Germany, offer a different and more serious ideological view of Andersen's tales based on artistic innovation. It is important not to exaggerate this dichotomy, for there are American films that are unusual artistic endeavors, and there are artificial European films made for the market of the culture industry. Yet, there are clear differences between European approaches to fairy-tale films for children and adults and those produced in America. It is also obvious that the control of the distribution of the films has played and will continue to play an important role with regard to who will win the struggle over Andersen's heritage. Most people do not even know that there is a struggle, and yet it has existed ever since his works were translated and distributed in other countries. The appropriation of Andersen's fairy tales and stories was something he both desired and feared, for he realized that his fame might shadow his real self and contribute to further misunderstanding of his poetic genius. For instance, Andersen's tales appear to the American public largely through a Disney or entertainment lens — as commodities, offered by a quaint Danish writer, to be consumed for enjoyment. Disney has overshadowed Andersen. There is an ethical problem in such adaptation that I shall discuss at the end of this chapter. But first I want to outline the discourse of cinematic appropriation as a struggle over Andersen's legacy before talking about ethics.

Only a select number of Andersen tales have been adapted for the cinema and TV in the West, and I want to analyze film adaptations of "The Little Mermaid," "The Princess on the Pea," "The Emperor's New Clothes," "The Swineherd," and "The Shepherdess and the Chimney Sweep" to reflect upon our predisposition to commemorate Andersen's work in the twenty-first century, exactly 200 years after his birth. Many of the Andersen films are not well known in the United States and the United Kingdom, and yet these "unknown" films inform the popular image and reception of Andersen in English-speaking countries. That is, the public is rarely informed about them.

Cinematic Adaptations

The Little Mermaid

Published in 1837, "The Little Mermaid," one of Andersen's most popular tales, has been adapted for film and television more often than any of his other works. The popularity of this tale may, in fact, have a great deal to do with the long history of European fascination with mermaids, often associated with sirens and water sprites. Myths, legends, and folk tales recounting the formidable power of mermaids can be traced back to Greek and Roman antiquity. Generally speaking, mermaids have always been regarded as dangerous because of their beauty and seductive voices, which they use to lure seamen to disaster and death. At the same time, many folk tales and legends feature mermaids who are more humane and long to possess a Christian soul. The classic example of this type of tale is Friedrich de La Motte-Fouqué's *Undine* (1811), in which a water sprite falls in love with a knight and can only marry him if she possesses a soul. After she makes a great sacrifice for the knight, Undine marries him, only to be betrayed. Andersen knew Fouqué's story and was clearly influenced by it. However, Andersen transformed the tale into a Christian miracle narrative that was intended to celebrate the power of Christian salvation.

In Denmark, most Andersen scholars now accept the view proposed by James Massengale that:

> "The Little Mermaid" concerns a miracle, rather than a simple matter of unrequited love and suicide which is followed by a bit of authorial "structuring invocation." This is not to say that there are no valid critical methods around that would deny the miracle issue. That would be silly. But it is no longer the case that those who accept Andersen's use of an integrally positioned and functionally necessary miracle will find themselves in an isolated periphery.[1]

By exploring the narrative perspective from the mermaid's behavior and desires, Massengale demonstrates convincingly that the young fifteen-year-old protagonist has been strongly influenced by her grandmother. She learns that she must suffer to gain a position in the upper world and that she can never gain an immortal soul. Her grandmother explains: "'We can live until we are three hundred years old; but when we die, we become the foam on the ocean. We cannot even bury our loved ones. We do not have immortal souls. When we die, we shall never rise again.'"[2] Disappointed, the mermaid responds, "'Why do I not have an immortal soul!... I would give all my three hundred years of life for one day as a human being if, afterward, I should be allowed to live in the heavenly world'" (p. 66).

Although the mermaid has fallen in love with the prince, it is not so much the young man whom she desires, but rather a Christian soul. Therefore, her task is twofold: she must learn what the mermen laws require so that she can barter her voice to become human; and she must learn the Christian principles of compliance with the laws of God based on compassion, charity, and self-sacrifice so that she can obtain a soul. Her story is not a coming-of-age story. It is a Christian conversion story based on a miracle: the pagan girl learns all about Christian love and devotion. Instead of dying at the end of the fairy tale, the mermaid miraculously becomes a daughter of the air, and the daughters, just like her grandmother, provide her with new rules of Christian instruction (pp. 75–6):

> "Mermaids have no immortal soul and can never have one, unless they can obtain the love of a human being. Their chance of obtaining eternal life depends upon others. We, daughters of the air, have not received an eternal soul either; but we can win one by good deeds. We fly to the warm countries, where the

The Little Mermaid (1846) illustrated by J. Leech in *Bentley's Miscellany*

heavy air of the plague rests, and blow cool winds to spread it. We carry the smell of flowers that refresh and heal the sick. If for three hundred years we earnestly try to do what is good, we obtain an immortal soul and can take part in the eternal happiness of man. You, little mermaid, have tried with all your

heart to do the same. You have suffered and borne your suffering bravely; and that is why you are now among us, the spirits
of the air. Do your good deeds and in three hundred years an
immortal soul will be yours."

It is important to recall that the prince never learns that it was the
mermaid who saved him. Nor does he fall in love with her. He is struck by
her devotion, and it is her devotion to him that entails self-sacrifice and
brings about her own miraculous salvation. There is some debate among
Danish scholars as to whether the salvation is Catholic or Lutheran. But
as Massengale points out, this debate is somewhat irrelevant because
Andersen really invents his own peculiar, mystical Christian salvation.
What is more relevant is the manner in which Andersen stylized the
legendary material to make it acceptable for bourgeois households in
Denmark, especially for children whose parents wanted them to learn
about virtuous behavior.

As we have seen, virtuous behavior in an Andersen tale almost always
requires self-submission: the dialogues are exchanges about power relations;
the omniscient narrator, while often ironic, rationalizes the behavior of
protagonists who alter their lives to be dominated or become a member
of the dominant class; and the ideology underlines the principles of divine
providence and faith in higher powers, often represented by a Christian
God. But "The Little Mermaid" is not only about Christian obedience,
virtue, and salvation. It is, from a feminist perspective, a misogynist tale
about dampening the sexual curiosity of a young female, who wants to
explore other worlds.[3] The mermaid must learn her proper place in the
order of things, and it is apparently improper for her to pursue a young
man, to express her sexual drives, and to change her social position. It is
not by chance that Andersen has her tongue cut out, and she feels as if her
legs were piercing her like swords when she walks. Once she turns human,
she enters a world totally dominated by male desire and has no choice but
to commit suicide. She realizes that she will never fit into a world that does
not accept her devotion, and murdering the prince will not bring her any
satisfaction. The contrived miracle is nothing but a false compensation for
a young woman who has lost hope in life and cannot fulfill her desires.
The tragedy of depression due to social oppression runs through Western
literature up to the present, and the hidden theme of female suicide in
fairy tales has been amply explored in Anne Sexton's *Transformations*, a
collection of provocative, poetical retellings of the Grimms' tales. Sexton,

The Little Mermaid (1846) illustrated by Joseph J. Mora in **Hans Andersen's Fairy Tales**

who committed suicide, depicts the bitter and tragic struggles of female protagonists who seek to break out of the confines of bourgeois domestic life, which she saw as a prison and a coffin. Andersen antedated Sexton by over 130 years, but he concealed his sadomasochism in tales that involved notions of self-effacement and punitive attitudes toward women. Yet, these themes are clearly elaborated in "The Little Mermaid," which can also be interpreted as a commentary about art and the artist.

If we understand the mermaid as a metaphorical representation of the artist, then Andersen is asking how the artist can articulate his desires and needs as well as his love of beauty in a public realm governed by patronage. This question is raised most poignantly in "The Nightingale," but "The Little Mermaid" prefigures that tale and outlines the dilemma of an artist, totally dependent on a prince who does not and cannot appreciate what she has to offer. Whereas the nightingale as singer survives and comes to an agreement with the emperor, the artist in "The Little Mermaid" loses her voice and cannot express why she is vital for the prince's life. She is miserable as a mime. She cannot dance without feeling pain. She cannot sing. At the court she is a mere ornament whose essence cannot be truly valued. She had deluded herself into believing that she could attract the prince through her art. What is there for her to do but to kill herself, thereby creating an artistic tragedy? Self-denial and abnegation constitute the suffering that informs many of Andersen's great masterpieces. His suffering and self-denial formed a well of experience that he exploited time and again to explain that he deserved more recognition than he was granted.

Far be it from the Disney Studios, however, to produce a film about suicide and abnegation for family audiences in 1989. *The Little Mermaid*, directed by Robert Clements and John Musker, is a coming-of-age story about a feisty "American" mermaid, who pouts and pushes until she gets her way: she is the charming, adorable, spoiled and talented princess, Daddy's pet, who demonstrates that she deserves to move up into the real world by dint of her perseverance and silence. Ariel must learn to channel her sexual desires and suffer for a man before she can win him as a prize, and — make no doubt about it — Eric, the prince, is a prize catch in the eyes of Americans young and old. There is nothing Danish or European about the Disney film, for Ariel and Eric are depicted as your typical American teenagers, and the film resembles more a Broadway or Hollywood musical than it does the serious religious fairy tale written by Andersen. In fact, the Disney film is an eternal-return-of-the-same romance about girl meets boy, girl falls for boy, boy falls for girl, evil forces prevent the virtuous youngsters from consummating their love, but love triumphs over evil, and the couple will live happily ever after.

This is a formula that Walt Disney developed with music and color animation in the early 1930s. *Snow White and the Seven Dwarfs* (1937) laid down the prescribed formula: Snow White and the prince fall in love through a song in the first scene of the film; an older woman as witch/queen despises Snow White and wants to eliminate her so that she can become the most powerful and beautiful queen in the land; Snow White's curiosity almost causes her death; the dwarfs defeat the witch; the prince revives Snow White. In *The Little Mermaid* the formula is almost exactly the same: Ariel spies the prince and falls in love with him; Ursula the sea witch hates her and her father and wants to destroy them and take over their kingdom; Ariel's curiosity and desire to be part of another world almost causes her death as well as her father's; the prince saves Ariel by piercing the witch with the phallic bow of his ship; thanks to him Ariel is retransformed from mermaid into a beautiful bride.

In many respects the Disney version of *The Little Mermaid* was the quintessential American film to close out a decade that had been largely determined by Hollywood spectacle and the reign of Ronald Reagan. The 1970s had been a decade of instability, violence, social upheaval, and the rise of mass movements for social reform. The 1980s began turning back the clock through self-healing, self-absorption, and the reintroduction of conservative values and practices. By 1989, even though the unromantic George H.W. Bush was in power, America was back in the romance mode of spectacle, entertainment, delusion, and anesthesia, and a film for the family, especially a Disney film, that might deal with religion, suicide, and death would not only have been a commercial failure, it would have been "sinful" and not in keeping with Disney corporate practices.

The Little Mermaid was indeed a success because it was true to the conventional Disney form and formula of animated fairy-tale films, and it is certainly not without its artistic merits. The songs are catchy; the humor, witty; the animation, effective. Ariel is a spunky heroine, who speaks and acts like a good, white, middle-class heroine of the 1980s. It is true that she sacrifices her voice and fins for the love of a man, but it should be noted that this gesture can be read as an acceptance of the "other," an overcoming of xenophobia, a celebration of her curiosity. Though she marries a prince who has a similar background to hers, Eric is not a member of the merfolk, and Ariel goes against her father's wishes when she pursues him. In other words, we have a mixed marriage in the end, an acceptance of the "other." Finally, as Laura Sells argues in an attempt to temper the feminist critique of the film:

> Even though Ariel has been complicit in the death of Ursula, and the destined alliance with patriarchy is fulfilled, I remain hopeful. After all, Ariel enters the white male system with her

voice — a stolen, flying voice that erupted amidst patriarchal language, a voice no longer innocent because it resided for a time in the dark continent that is the Medusa's home.[4]

Sells wrote these comments before *The Little Mermaid* sequels appeared, and more than likely her hope for Ariel has been disappointed. Ariel's temporary nonconformist behavior was basically a selling point in the Disney film; her rebellion was never to be taken seriously because she was destined from the beginning to wed the perfect partner and form a charming couple that would beget not a only a baby, but a TV series of *The Little Mermaid* (1992–94), and a sequel, *The Little Mermaid II: The Return to the Sea* (2000). The underlying principle of the Disney corporate production of films is to seek topics that will sell the same message in slightly different packaging to advertise the brand name of their products. The second feature film is basically a repeat of the first one, but much duller. This film should have been titled: "Return to the Fold." It concerns little Melody, the twelve-year-old daughter, spawned by Ariel and Eric. They try to keep her away from the sea because she was threatened by the witch Morgana, Ursula's sister, when she was a baby. Yet, Melody has a natural inclination for the water, rebels against her mother, and is duped by Morgana, who pretends to support her rebellion and appears to be a mother substitute. Melody steals the magic scepter of her grandfather, King Triton, and all hell breaks lose. Once Melody realizes how destructive she has become, she steals the scepter back from Morgana, who becomes imprisoned in ice for the rest of her life. Melody is reconciled with her parents, and they will undoubtedly live happily ever after.

The trite story involves a traditional mother-daughter conflict: Ariel is overly protective, and Melody does not understand why her mother wants to keep her from the sea. Her anger is misdirected at Ariel, and therefore, she must learn the error of her ways. So the film's simple message is about corrective behavior: the daughter must learn to trust her mother, and the mother must learn to trust her daughter. All's well that ends well. On a positive note, the film offers a critique of the "me-generation" of the 1990s, an antidote to the narcissism of the young. However, serious questions about social attitudes and political power struggles are rarely treated with depth in Disney fairy-tale films, especially the Andersen adaptations. Whereas Andersen's tale is disturbing and ambivalent about the meaning of happiness, Disney's *The Little Mermaid* films are sentimental, romantic, and one-dimensional. Happiness is there for the grabbing. One just needs will power (and perhaps a little help from rich and powerful dads and grand-dads.) In both feature films, there is also an interesting hidden motif that is played down (or under) and needs to be explored because of its significance in most of the Disney and American fairy-tale films. It is the question of male hegemony: Triton appears in both of Disney's *The Little Mermaid* films as a powerful, benevolent ruler, who is gentle and uses his phallic scepter for the good of the multicolored merfolk. His reign is always threatened by dark female witches, Ursula and Morgana, who are projected as slithery octopuses with tentacles grabbing for power. What are we to make of this black-and-white image of the gender power struggle? What are we to make out of the contrast between the dark witches and the white fairy heroines Ariel and Melody, who are lovely, innocent, and sweet? The harmonious endings of both films suggest that we, the audience, are not to think any more about evil associated with women and blackness, just as long as the magic scepter is in Triton's hands.

The dramatic conflict between the kind king Triton and the wicked sea witches Ursula and Morgana is totally lacking in the Faerie Tale Theatre production, *The Little Mermaid* (1987), directed by Robert Iscove. So are the humor and the music. The twenty-seven films in the Faerie Tale Theatre series, produced by the actress Shelly Duvall, are basically venues for celebrity actors and directors to have some "fun" with classic fairy tales. Between 1982 and 1987 Duvall hired many of her acquaintances in Hollywood to try their hand at adapting fairy tales in innovative ways and to show the results on TV or in homes as videotapes. As might be expected, the films are uneven, largely because the fairy tales are a means for the actors to show off their talents and to tweak the tales in titillating ways. Some manage to be serious and artistic and endeavor to offer relevant observations on the Andersen texts for contemporary audiences.

Iscove's *The Little Mermaid*, is, however, one of the least stimulating of the live-action films in the series. In fact, it is downright tedious. Unlike the Disney adaptation of the Andersen tale, this film sticks fairly close to the original narrative, though it drops the Christian themes and motifs. The film is narrated by Neptune, the little mermaid's father, and the girl is anything but little: she is called Pearl and turns twenty-one at the beginning of story. After a brief celebration of her birthday, she is allowed to rise to the top of the ocean for twenty-four hours. During this time she falls in love with a sailor prince named Andrew, saves his life, and returns to the bottom of the ocean, where she visits an outspoken, wry sea witch, who gives her legs. But she also takes away her voice and tells Pearl that she will turn into sea foam unless the prince falls in love with her and marries her. When she returns to land as a human, Pearl discovers that the prince, who is fond of her like a little pet or sister, is in love with Princess Amelia. In fact, he marries her, and Pearl's sister is despondent because Pearl will have to become sea foam. However, Pearl's sisters surface with a knife and encourage her to kill the prince so she can regain her mermaid form. Pearl resists and turns into a sea spirit, not sea foam. Neptune, the omniscient narrator, appears to believe that this is a grand accomplishment of some sort, and the film ends on a bittersweet note and a view of the ocean.

The tragedy of the film has nothing to do with the mermaid's fate but with the tedium and meaninglessness of the adaptation. Pearl has no personality whatsoever, and her rebellion is virtually placid. The sea witch, played by the well-known comic actress Karen Black, endeavors to add some spark to the film, but her American slang and corny jokes fall flat. It is a trademark of the Duvall fairy-tale films that the characters often speak with British, American, Irish, and regional accents in the same setting; this is supposed to be cute and comic, but it adds very little to the characterization of the particular people and detracts from the action and meaning of the film. One is supposed to suspend one's imagination while watching a fairy-tale film, but the suspension cannot work if the art is banal. The prince, who is depicted as the typical prince charming, is too virtuous to be true, and though there is some dramatic tension between Princess Amelia and Pearl, the acting is so predictable that few spectators can be moved by Pearl's death after the marriage of Amelia and Andrew.

There are other American adaptations of "The Little Mermaid" that follow the same schemes of the Disney and Duvall versions, but they are not worth reviewing because they are so imitative. The difficulties that most of these films have is related to their effort to make Andersen's tales appropriate for the children and the family "market" while introducing new elements that will draw people to "consume" the films. "Appropriate" generally means simplistic and moralistic. The morals of the American fairy-tale films tend to be clear and easy to grasp, and there can never be real tragedy or exploration of sexuality and politics. Though European films often follow the same pattern, there are some important exceptions, especially because the European directors often add complex philosophical and ideological aspects to their films. Moreover, European films were not always produced to pander to a commercial market. In some cases,

The Little Mermaid (1893) illustrated by J. R. Weguelin in *The Little Mermaid and Other Stories*

they were conceived as a means of avoiding censorship while providing a political critique of a totalitarian state.

One of the most intriguing cinematic adaptations of Andersen's "The Little Mermaid" is the Russian director Vladimir Bychko's *Rusalochka* (1976). Set in the nineteenth century, the film begins in a large coach traveling through the countryside. A man with a top hat and beard, who resembles Andersen in his forties, gazes at a young woman, blonde and fragile, who is evidently disturbed by something. To cheer her up, the traveler/Andersen tells her an unusual version of "The Little Mermaid," in which he assumes the role of Sulpicius, a poet, and the young woman, the role of the mermaid.

The traveler/Andersen sets his story in the late medieval period; the landscape is barren and rough, and the stone dwellings and castle are solid but not particularly beautiful or splendid. A foreign ship is off at sea, where the birthday of the prince is being celebrated. He gazes into the sea and notices the mermaid, who bedazzles him, and it appears that the sailors are also bewitched. The ship runs aground on rocks and must be abandoned. The mermaid saves the prince and deposits him on the beach in a safe place. The princess of the kingdom, who is a cold and opportunistic person, happens to come by with her ladies-in-waiting, and they bring the prince back to her castle.

The mermaid, struck by love, wants to see the prince again and manages to swim up to the moat of the castle. When some men see her, they want to harm her because mermaids are associated with the devil. She avoids them and encounters the poet Sulpicius, to whom she reveals her love for the prince. In turn, he warns her to avoid people and return to the sea. However, she is so desperately in love that Sulpicius promises to help her. He fetches a witch, who is an innkeeper, and the witch gives her legs and takes away her hair. She tells her that she will die from love if the prince marries someone else. In that event, the only way she can be saved is if someone sacrifices his life for her.

What is interesting in this story is that the mermaid retains her voice, and whenever she is confronted and questioned about her intentions and identity, she always tells the truth. Thus she is persecuted constantly as an outsider, a stranger who cannot adjust to the intolerant populace and the artificiality of court life. Sulpicius manages to save her time and again, but the prince, who becomes involved in a duel with an insidious prince over the hand of the cold princess, does not have much integrity and ignores the mermaid's love. Even when he learns that the princess has been deceitful, he still feels he must honor the chivalric code and marry her. This marriage will kill the mermaid, who tries to overcome her sadness and despondency by dancing on his wedding night. The next day, a masked man challenges the prince to a duel in behalf of the mermaid, and the prince kills him. When the mask is taken off the man, we see that it is Sulpicius, who has sacrificed his life to save the mermaid, who turns into an immortal dream. Then the story returns to the coach with the traveler/Andersen and the young woman, who appears to have regained her composure, and the coach travels on.

Bychko packs this film with several important interrelated themes. The major one concerns identity. Throughout the film, even though her form changes, the mermaid guards the integrity of her feelings, which are sincere and candid. She wards off the cruelty of the superstitious soldiers and peasants and cannot be corrupted by the court society. Her innocence is protected by the poet Sulpicius, who grasps the danger of her situation and protects her until he realizes that he can only save her by sacrificing his own life. As the figure of ineffable innocence and honesty, the mermaid's identity cannot be determined by other people who want to brand her as siren, witch, devil, pet, angel, and so on. Her actions speak for her character, and her character reveals the ugly sides of a society that is hollow and barbaric. The social codes of the court and the religious beliefs are exposed by the mermaid, who in some ways is almost a Christ figure, for she remains gentle and compassionate throughout her adventures in a world that is foreign to her. If Sulpicius represents the power of art, then the film appears to say that its function is to save integrity and truth during a time of social and political degeneration.

Unlike the American cinematic versions of "The Little Mermaid," Bychko's film takes Andersen's tale more seriously philosophically and ideologically to explore issues of class struggle, identity, love, and religion in innovative ways. In fact, the film also seeks to make a comment on the poetics of Andersen, the storyteller. Unlike the Faerie Tale Theatre film, in which Neptune does not play a role in the action and benignly blesses his daughter, the narrator Andersen becomes immersed in the tale he narrates: the storyteller tells his tale out of compassion for his listener, and it is his love for her that spurs the story, which is intended to strike a chord in her heart. Art is not designed for consumption, but to arouse the feelings of the audience, to inspire people to contemplate their ontological situation. It is also very personal, as was Andersen's art. But the Russian director is not so much interested in capturing Andersen's "true" personal situation as artist, instead addressing the personal and political situations in his own times. If Soviet society in the 1970s was unfeeling and bigoted, censored artists had to be clever storytellers, and they often used fairy-tale materials to reflect deeply upon the hypocrisy of the state and what effect its policies had on the people.

The Princess on the Pea

Another remarkable Russian fairy-tale film produced in 1976 was Boris Rytsarev's *The Princess on the Pea*, which makes use of five different fairy tales by Andersen. "The Princess on the Pea" (1835) was one of Andersen's first tales; it is very short, brisk, and ironic. The narrator informs us that there was once a prince who wanted to marry a real princess. He travels the whole world looking for one without success. So he returns home, sad and despondent, and evidently withdraws from society because he does not appear again until the very end of the story. In the meantime, a "real" princess arrives one night during a storm. The king himself lets her into the palace. He and his wife do not believe she is a real princess. They give her a test by placing a pea beneath twenty mattresses to see how sensitive she is. She passes the test by informing them that she was not able to sleep the entire night and is black and blue all over. The prince marries her, and the pea is placed in the royal museum. The narrator comments that we can go and see it if it hasn't been stolen and exclaims, "Now that was a real story!" (p. 20).

What is real is associated with true, authentic, and pure. It may also be associated with blood. As we know, there is a strong essentialist streak in many of Andersen's stories. One is often brilliant, handsome, and genial and born into nobility, as is the case with the ugly duckling. The prince plays a very minor role in the tale, and the irony is that he could have found what he sought if he had just remained at home. Andersen's delightful tale is somewhat simplistic and simple, but it has served as the frame for more profound elaboration.

Rytsarev's treatment is one of the more original and imaginative explorations of "The Princess on the Pea." He introduces three other Andersen tales ("The Swineherd," "The Traveling Companion," and "The Most Incredible") into the frame by having the king send the prince out into the world the morning after the "real" princess arrives during a nocturnal storm. The king and queen, not very wealthy, had become desperate to find the right princess for their son and had even placed a sign in front of their castle: "Princess Wanted." They did not believe that the young woman who had arrived during the night was truly a princess, which is why the prince sets off on his travels before he can get to know her.

Rytsarev transforms Andersen's fairy tale into a story about the education of a young prince in three stages. His first stop is at a castle, where he views a beautiful but arrogant princess, who values artificiality over natural beauty. The prince exchanges roles with a swineherd and attempts to win the princess's affection, only to learn how supercilious she is, and he returns her arrogance by humiliating her. The second stop is at a castle where another beautiful princess says that she will marry any suitor who can guess the answer to three riddles. The suitors who fail are beheaded. The prince discovers that she is in love with a troll, but the princess is afraid to admit this to her father, who wants her to find a husband. The father does not realize that a troll is providing the princess with the riddles so that they can get rid of her suitors and continue to meet in secret. However, the prince reveals their secret and actually brings about their union. His third stop is at a kingdom where a princess promises her hand in marriage to the artist who produces the most superb work of art. The prince manages to create a magnificent rose in a luminous vase, but a ferocious knight suddenly arrives and mocks his art by destroying it. The princess is awed by the knight, and he carries her off to the castle. After these three encounters, the prince returns forlorn to his castle. To his surprise, he sees that the princess, whom he does not believe is a princess, is still there and has won the affection of his mother and father. The prince, who has grown during his journey, can now see how honest, genuine, and natural she is, especially compared with the princesses he has met. Finally, his mother and father try the pea test to see whether she is truly a princess. She passes the test. Later, a merchant purchases the pea and places it in a museum.

The question of authenticity is central for Rytsarev. The pea test is incidental, and it only verifies what everyone already knows: the princess is a genuine person. The status of her royalty does not really mean anything. The vision of the prince and his mother and father has to be corrected so that they can appreciate values such as sincerity, modesty, honesty, and so on. On each of the encounters during his journey, the prince learns to recognize that beauty and social rank can be deceptive. Rytsarev's sets and costumes are created to emphasize the difference between artificial spectacle and the beauty of simplicity. The prince is constantly placed in the position of an outsider looking into and beneath the veneer of beauty represented by the princess. Moreover, Rytsarev brings out different perspectives with regard to authenticity by drawing on three other Andersen tales and exploring their meanings in unusual ways, thereby enabling us to see how Andersen himself was constantly seeking to establish what constitutes the nature of authentic art, a theme that is most productively treated in "The Nightingale."

In Andersen's "The Princess on the Pea," sensitivity was the standard by which one was to judge "realness" or authenticity. In Rytsarev's film, however, there are many more standards, for the prince as critic is educated first to dismiss artificiality, deception, and pretension. His eyes are opened, and by virtue of insight, he can begin to determine what constitutes beauty. The princess he chooses is physically not the most beautiful of women, but she is the most natural; there is nothing deceptive or pretentious about her. She is disarming because she is so forthright and reveals the extraordinary in the ordinary. This was a key artistic principle in Andersen's style that Rytsarev develops, for it is through the prince's eyes that spectators come to appreciate the beauty of natural simplicity and candor.

In the Faerie Tale Theatre production of *The Princess and the Pea* (1984), directed by Tony Bill, there is a similar attempt to explore the meaning of authenticity, but the slapstick humor, mixed accents, and stupid sexism undermine the defense of simplicity and gentleness. Nevertheless, the frame of the story is interesting: a custodian in a nineteenth-century museum explains to a bungling married couple the significance of a pea in a glass case by telling the story of "The Princess on the Pea." The custodian becomes the royal fool, and the man and wife become the pompous king and queen, who are also vain and superficial. Their son, played by the British actor Tom Conti, is not much better: he is naïve, spoiled, and ignorant. He wants a pet for a friend and is convinced by the court fool that a wife would be better than an animal. Therefore, he asks his parents to provide a wife, and they agree to find one providing that she is a real princess. By coincidence, a princess, played by Liza Minelli with an American accent and verve, appears out of a storm. She is admitted into the castle by the prince, who hides her in the fool's room to keep an ordinary girl out of the sight of his parents, for he does not believe she is a real princess. One of the first things she does is to clean the fool's room to show she has the talents of a good housewife. Then she gives the prince sound advice each time he is introduced to prospective brides, who are either pretentious or opportunistic. Finally, he realizes he is in love with the gentle, sincere princess, whom he has been concealing. Once she is submitted to the pea test, she passes, to his pleasant surprise, and they marry, although one must wonder why she would wed such a self-absorbed, simple-minded man.

The answer, of course, is that the director and actors are just having fun with the tale, creating entertainment for audiences, who are not supposed to think about the complex nature of authenticity. A good, clean-cut girl as pet for the prince provides the answer to his boredom, a girl whom he will be able to control because she is so malleable. If one of the dominant messages in the classical fairy tales from the seventeenth century to the twentieth century was the domestication of beautiful girls, who were celebrated for their compliance, then this 1984 cinematic version does not reflect much about the transformation of women's roles in society. According to the film, the "authentic" princess is the authentic house cleaner and pet, who knows her proper place.

The Swineherd

This message is also prominent in the West German filmmaker Herbert Fredersdorf's adaptation of "The Swineherd," one of Andersen's most satiric fairy tales that also deals with the question of authenticity. In Andersen's brief narrative, a poor prince courts a supercilious princess and sends her a beautiful rose and a nightingale with a marvelous voice. However, she rejects them because they are real. So the prince disguises himself as a swineherd and captivates her with a marvelous pot that plays divine music. She must pay the prince ten kisses for the pot. Then he creates a rattle that plays all the waltzes and dances of the world. Again she ardently desires to possess the rattle, but the prince now demands 100 kisses, which, after hesitating, she eventually agrees to give him. This time, however, her father, the emperor, catches them in the act, and he banishes her from the empire. As for the prince, he declares, "I have come to despise you.... You did not want an honest prince. You did not appreciate the rose or the nightingale, but you could kiss a swineherd for the sake of a toy. Farewell!" (p. 197). He closes the door to the kingdom, and the princess is left with nothing.

As usual, Andersen criticizes the upper class for its artificial values. To be more precise, he uses a female figure as he did in "The Little Mermaid" and "The Red Shoes" to embody superficiality and fickleness. The overt sexist portrayal was common in Andersen's times and can be found in the fairy tales of other writers such as "King Thrushbeard" by the Brothers Grimm, who often subscribed to the motto: shrews must be tamed, and even innocent girls must be taught brutal lessons. In Andersen, females are often tamed as well as humiliated and tortured. In "The Swineherd," he punishes the princess severely because she has no aesthetic appreciation and enjoys petty, worthless objects. There can be no redemption for her.

The Swineherd (1887) illustrated by Joseph J. Mora in *Hans Andersen's Fairy Tales*

In contrast, Fredersdorf has some compassion for the princess. After all, he created this film shortly after the end of World War II, and he apparently wanted to create a fairy-tale film for family audiences that radiated with forgiveness and harmony. His changes to the plot are minor but significant. He adds a court jester named Hick to the cast of characters, and this fool intercedes on behalf of Prince Honestheart, who disguises himself as a swineherd working at the palace of Princess Rosemouth after she rejects his beautiful gifts. Indeed, the new swineherd makes a great impression on her and her father when he cleans up the pigsty and is always clean-cut himself. As in Andersen's tale, he invents two toys that enchant her, and after the king discovers their kissing act, he banishes her. However, the prince knows that she, too, has a good heart and must only learn a lesson in humiliation. So he informs the king, through Hick the jester, of his true identity as a prince. The princess is led to believe that she must marry the swineherd and succumbs to her fate. Yet in this cinematic version of Andersen's tale, her fate is a royal reward: she marries the prince, and the king ironically remarks in the end: "Such a good swineherd I'll never be able to find."

While there is a great deal of irony in the film thanks to an intrusive narrator, who is also corny and foolish, the storyline basically follows the traditional plot of sentimental romance. The film does not address the question about authentic versus false art. The major question pertains to the transformation of a spoiled princess. In this regard, Fredersdorf, who produced other fairy-tale films during this time, follows a tendency in West German filmmaking to produce happy-end films that would not disturb postwar audiences, especially children. Conflict was to be avoided or sugar-coated, and reconciliation of differences was to be fostered. It was also important to put women in their proper place, especially since many had joined the workforce during World War II and had become independent. While Andersen punished women for forgetting their proper roles in his fairy tales, the German Fredersdorf uses Andersen to slap them on their wrists and promise them a better future. Their authentic role calls for submission to both father and husband.

The Nightingale

Another Faerie Tale Theatre production that deals with authenticity is *The Nightingale*, starring Mick Jagger and Barbara Hershey, narrated by Shelly Duvall, and directed by Ivan Passer. Andersen's tale is perhaps one of his most profound meditations on the nature of art and patronage. The mighty Chinese emperor goes through a learning process and realizes that the pure and natural music of the nightingale is more valuable for his well-being than a beautifully ornamented mechanical bird that has no feeling for his life and becomes useless when it breaks down. The quality of authentic art for Andersen depends on the freedom granted the artist in the patronage system. The nightingale produces magnificent music that enthralls the emperor and his court, and it does so out of genuine affection for the emperor, who will die if he cannot hear such exotic music, that is, pleasurable art that is a life force and provides meaning in life. Art from an ordinary-looking bird can only endure if there is mutual affection and respect.

This is the basic message of Passer's *The Nightingale,* but there are some additional flourishes added to the plot that makes this film one of the more unique and successful productions in the Faerie Tale Theatre series. The major protagonist in the film is not the emperor of Cathay or the nightingale, but the kitchen maid. It is she who discovers the nightingale in the forest while she is looking for a root that will heal her sick grandmother. When the emperor hears about the exquisite nightingale, it is she who leads the courtiers to bring the bird back from the forest to their ruler. Finally, after the nightingale is banished by the austere emperor, who is about to die, it is the kitchen maid who pleads with the nightingale in the forest to return to the court and save the emperor's life. In the end, it is the emperor's discovery of the kitchen maid's heroic actions that brings him happiness and makes him realize how false and pretentious his court and courtiers are.

Passer's cinematic adaptation of "The Nightingale" remains close to the text. The Oriental setting and costumes are lavish, and they are contrasted with the more natural setting outside the palace and in the forest. The courtiers are much too foppish throughout the film, and the emperor appears to bathe in their flattery. His seclusion from the outside world has apparently contributed to his narrow appreciation of beauty. Once again, in keeping with Andersen, it is the simplicity of art, the extraordinary nature of the ordinary, that is virtuous because it can heal the soul and make one aware of what is essential in life.

This is also the message of the famous Czech film, *The Emperor's Nightingale* (1948), directed by Jiri Trnka and Jiri Brdecka, who also wrote the screenplay. Trnka was one of the foremost puppeteers and illustrators in Europe, and the design, setting, and puppets for this live-action/animated film are highly imaginative, as is the plot. The story is set in contemporary Czechoslovakia, that is, the late 1940s, and a rich boy in a sailor suit is to celebrate his birthday in a huge mansion. However, instead of being happy, he is sad because his parents are not present, and he is prohibited from leaving the grounds by a huge steel fence and wall that surrounds the property. A little girl about the same age, perhaps nine or ten, wants to play ball with him, but he cannot leave the grounds. The celebration of his birthday is a disaster, and in the evening, he has a dream about the Chinese emperor. At this point, the animation begins, and we are transported to China where the emperor leads an extremely regimented life that suffocates him. It is not until a little girl brings him a nightingale that he begins to breathe and feel free. It is thanks to her music and the friendship of the little bird that he begins to break with custom and routine to lead a more spontaneous and natural life. When the boy awakens the next morning, he immediately realizes the meaning of the dream, gets dressed, and runs outside. The film ends with a shot of him climbing over the fence to join the girl, who leads him into the nearby woods.

Trnka and Brdecka created this film immediately following World War II, when Czechoslovakia was undergoing massive social and political changes. Therefore, the emphasis in this film is not so much on the authenticity of art, but how art can emancipate people from senseless tradition, strictures, and regimentation. Both the boy and the emperor are incarcerated; they yearn for a different kind of life. It is through the dream sequences, for the boy, and through the music and companionship of the bird, for the emperor, that they come to the realization that they have it within themselves to transform their lives. What makes this film especially effective and poetic is that no words are spoken. The action is narrated by a storyteller — and it is interesting to note that in the English version of 1951, the narrator is the brilliant actor Boris Karloff — and there is unusual lyrical music throughout the film. Unlike many live-action/animated films, there is no romance, no sentimentality. Rather, Andersen's tale is used to explore psychologically the suffering of an abandoned child, and how the imaginative power of art can work therapeutically to overcome depression brought about by containment and restrictions.

The Emperor's New Clothes

Clearly, Andersen's own tales have a substantial psychological dimension, and if it were not for his peculiar therapeutic art, the creation of tales for his well-being, he himself might have died from the suffering he endured. So it is not so much the artist's giving of himself to a patron in the hope of gaining a proper estimation of his creative talents — although this is important — that is crucial for Andersen's survival, but it is more what his art brought to himself so that he could maintain a vital equilibrium. Andersen's anger at a pretentious and indifferent upper class that lacked

The Emperor's New Clothes (1887) illustrated by Joseph J. Mora in *Hans Andersen's Fairy Tales*

sensitivity for art, especially for his particular kind of art, had to be channeled in such a way that he would not become self-destructive. This is most clear in the short poignant tale "The Emperor's New Clothes," which is not only an exposure of the foibles of the aristocracy, but also a critique of their aesthetic taste and false art. Unlike the Chinese emperor in "The Nightingale," the emperor in this tale is consumed by his fondness for new clothes. In fact, clothes are his fetish, for he has an outfit for every hour of the day. "Clothes make the person" is obviously his motto, and therefore, he is easy prey when the swindlers arrive and announce that they can weave a marvelous and beautiful cloth that "had the strange quality of being invisible to anyone who was unfit for his office or unforgivably stupid" (p. 77). The duping of the emperor and his courtiers is Andersen's critique of the Danish aristocracy, easily swindled by false artists who know nothing about the true nature of art. However, the swindlers do know a great deal about fashion and fetishism. They know how to market useless wares. They know all about the gullibility of people who presume to be connoisseurs. Andersen once again raises the question about what constitutes authentic art and its appreciation, and his narrative has a bittersweet taste of revenge at the end. The emperor, though he knows that he has been exposed, maintains the pretense and walks even more proudly to finish the procession. It is an open question as to whether the emperor has learned anything or will change. Certainly, he will be more alert in the future. Andersen's tale, which is not a fairy tale per se, is a satirical presentation of a pompous and narcissistic emperor, surrounded by sycophants. He is literally undressed so that he will expose himself as a fraud. What is interesting is that the swindlers serve truth, and we never learn what happens to them. Do we need deceivers to learn the truth about decadent and deceptive emperors? Or, do we need childlike honesty? Will the emperor be toppled by the people after they learn the truth? The tale raises as many questions as it answers and remains open-ended — an attack, an interrogation, an exposure.

The open end allows for many possible interpretations and interesting possibilities for artists who have sought to adapt the tale. The American film versions of Andersen's story have been more drawn to the character of the swindlers and have tended to emphasize the comic aspect of the emperor's exposure to the truth that he wants to keep from himself. Moreover, some have added romance to the plot, totally changing the signification of Andersen's story. Instead of a tale about decadent rule and the tasteless aesthetics of a king who is consumed by his own "beauty," the films, with one exception, minimize the effects that the ruler has on the people of his kingdom and generally makes light of the greed and hypocrisy of the emperor. The "heroes" of the tale are the swindlers, who are warm-hearted rascals and are appealing because they use their cunning to survive and rob the rich.

The first American rendition of "The Emperor's New Clothes" was an ABC television special in 1972 that capitalized on Danny Kaye's fame as Hans Christian Andersen. This version was filmed in a small town in Denmark with Kaye as the narrator dragging children about the town and speaking to an American TV audience about the quaintness of the Danish village. At one point he gathers the children around him, just as he had done in the film Hans Christian Andersen, and after donning the top hat of a swindler, he explains that it is part of a story that he begins to tell, one that is performed by puppets in cell animation and animagic as he narrates it. Unlike Andersen's tale, the major characters are the swindlers Marmaduke (voiced by Kaye) and his companion Musty (Alan Swift), who decide to seek the reward of one million grinklens by making extraordinary new clothes for Emperor Klonkenlocker (Cyril Ritchard). Little do they know that the court jester Jaspar (Robert McFadden) has been robbing the emperor and intends to marry his daughter Princess Klonkenlocker (Imogene Coca), who has another preferred suitor. In this version the questions of art and authenticity are secondary to those of greed and justice. The swindlers are basically good-hearted souls; the emperor, a good-natured but misguided ruler; and the jester, a conniving thief. Nothing is what it seems to be, and ironically the swindlers must correct the vision of the emperor and his subjects so that they can set everything right.

The puppetry in this film is superb. The movement is fluid, and the expressions are synchronized perfectly to make the behavior of the puppets credible; the costumes are colorful, and voice-overs by the actors lend depth to the personalities of the characters. The element of play is maintained throughout the film: Kaye is playing with the audience and the children in the film; the puppets are playing at being real people; the swindlers play at deceiving the emperor. If at times Kaye himself borders on being too sweet and infantile, he does not cross the line into meaningless humor. It is the gentle Kaye who guides us through a gentle romantic version of "The Emperor's New Clothes" and it is through his humor that we grasp how cunning swindlers can sometimes help us to discover the truth of a situation.

The 1987 Cannon production, *The Emperor's New Clothes*, directed by David Irving, endeavors to create the same kind of gentle entertainment in a live-action film but ultimately fails. In 1986–87 the producers Menahem Golan and Yoram Globus hurriedly made six fairy-tale films called *Canon Movie-Tales*, evidently in an effort to compete with Shelly Duvall's *Faerie Tale Theatre*. For the most part, the results are disastrous.

Though some of the films have unique and original elements, they all follow the same formula that combines the Disney and Hollywood musicals with sentimental plots that add very little to our understanding of the original fairy tales, and if anything, makes them seem trite.

It appears that Irving may have been familiar with the ABC television version of "The Emperor's New Clothes." The emperor, played by the inimitable comedian Sid Caesar, is obsessed by clothes, and he wants to have a splendid garment made for himself to celebrate the forthcoming wedding of his daughter Gilda, who is being forced to marry an insipid, ugly prince named Prince Nino because of his wealth. The two swindlers, a cunning rogue named Henry and his handsome nephew Nicholas, arrive and deceive the emperor and his foppish courtiers by promising to make a garment spun from his own jewels. Those who are not worthy of their station will not be able to see the new clothes. As they are making a gown out of thin air that the emperor and his advisers pretend to see so as not to reveal their unworthiness, Gilda falls in love with the charming Nicholas and conspires with the swindlers to avoid marriage with Prince Nino. In the end, Gilda elopes with Nicholas. The roguish Henry escapes but foolishly loses the jewels he has stolen. The emperor is exposed, but he is none the wiser, for it appears he will continue to have his clothes fetish.

The acting in the film is ludicrous, and if there is any meaning to the adaptation, it is lost in the slapstick comedy. In fact, the Andersen tale appears to be simply a vehicle for actors to clown about in a traditional romantic comedy that depicts how true love can triumph despite a father's stupidity, greedy courtiers, and crafty statesmen. The quality of the film, which has extravagant settings and costumes, is so poor that it does not even reach the level of camp because it is also predictable and boring. Perhaps it can be considered an achievement to transform an Andersen fairy tale into a boring film that reflects little upon the tale and reflects poorly on the marketing policy of its producers.

In contrast to the Cannon movie, the Faerie Tale Theatre production of *The Emperor's New Clothes* (1985), directed by Peter Medak, is unusually creative and raises some important social and political questions. The costumes and sets in this production are designed to bring out the difference between the social classes: the king and his court wear lavish clothes in baroque parlors, while the lower classes are dressed in tattered clothes, as are the two swindlers, Morty (Art Carney) and Bo (Alan Arkin). But before the two hucksters are introduced, we are treated to a highly comic spectacle of the emperor (Dick Shawn), who admires himself in mirrors and then treats his subjects to a mock fashion show. He strolls up and down a platform to the applause of his court and the people, whom he has taxed to support his extravagance. Soon thereafter the scene switches to Morty and Bo on the outskirts of the city. They speak in slang with New York accents, and Morty tells Bo that he wants to quit the fraud business, settle down, and set up a duck farm. All these plans are put on the back burner when they enter the town and learn of the emperor's fetish for clothes. Bo convinces Morty to pull off one more swindle before they become "honest."

The plot of the film follows the Andersen story closely from this point on, with one major exception: Morty and Bo encounter an innkeeper, who reveals how she might lose her inn and how heavily the people of the land are being taxed. In fact, conditions are so bad that the army consists of only one preposterous soldier, and the people have very little to eat. Consequently, Morty decides to take the emperor for all he is worth and to give the money and jewels to the innkeeper to share with the people. When the emperor is exposed by a little boy and driven from the town. Morty and Bo make off with enough gold to start a duck farm. Soon thereafter, the emperor returns to the kingdom, and having learned his lesson, he holds court in modest attire and begins to give money to the needy.

Although the ending with the transformation of the emperor appears to be tagged on, the changes made to Andersen's tale in this film, which is enriched by the stellar performances of Shawn, Arkin, and Carney, provide more substance to the tale. Whereas Andersen never reveals the impact of the emperor's extravagance on the people, Medak's film shows the poverty of the people, who are highly critical of the emperor. While Andersen was concerned with the authenticity of art and sought to convince the aristocracy that there was virtue in honesty and simplicity, Medak shifts the focus to questions of government, social injustice, and reform — questions that were appropriate during the Reagan regime in America during the 1980s, for Reagan's inner government was stylized as a Hollywood court. These serious questions are also at the bottom of what I consider the most probing and most profound cinematic adaptation of an Andersen tale.

The Shepherdess and the Chimney Sweep

Although Andersen's tale of a beautiful shepherdess and a handsome chimney sweep is not well-known in the United States and much

Mr. Bird rescuing his son on top of a statue of the king in Paul Grimault's
Le Roi et l'Oiseau **(1979)**

of Europe, it has become extremely popular in France through the brilliant cinematic work of Paul Grimault, who actually made two versions, *La Bergère et le ramoneur* (1950; English version, *The Curious Adventures of Mr. Wonderbird*, 1952)[5] and *Le Roi et l'Oiseau* (*The King and the Bird*, 1979), which does not have an English version. In both films he collaborated with the unique poet and screenplay writer, Jacques Prévert.

Andersen's tale, as we have seen, can be interpreted as a story about the fear of freedom. The shepherdess and the chimney sweep are awed by the outside world and return to the safe and comfortable parlor, where they

The cross-eyed king in Paul Grimault's *Le Roi et l'Oiseau* (1979)

submit to its social code. Only by accident do they become happy, if they really do become happy. In contrast, Grimault's two films can be regarded as odes to freedom. In both renditions he celebrates the emancipation not only of the persecuted couple from a mean-spirited dictator, but also the freedom of the oppressed populace living in darkness. First conceived in 1945, Grimault's two films hark back to World War II, the French occupation by the Nazis, and the atomic bomb. These events marked Grimault and Prévert to such an extent that they worked on the project for twenty-four years until they made the film as they desired and envisaged it. Because the 1979 version was Grimault's "final" statement about Andersen's

"The Shepherdess and the Chimney Sweep," I want to summarize the plot of this film, written with Prévert, who died right before the final production, before examining how imaginatively he interpreted Andersen's work and contributed to the development of animation.

The film begins with the depiction of a cross-eyed vain king, who rules a mythical urban state modeled after a feudal kingdom and a quaint futuristic realm. The king's apparent hierarchical and authoritarian reign is reflected by the total submission of his subjects and the many pictures, statues, and designs that have his face on it. He is about to go hunting, his greatest avocation, and just when one of his servants sets free a tiny cute bird (the target of the hunt) from a diminutive cage, a large crowlike bird with a top hat and vest suddenly swoops down and saves the tiny one. It is his son, and he taunts the king, who had recently shot and killed his wife.

The king is furious and retires to his royal apartments, which are on top of a 96-story building. One can only gain access to his rooms by a super-powered elevator. Once there, he has another portrait in hunting attire made for himself and then executes the artist for making the painting too accurate by showing his crossed eyes. (Throughout the film, the king pushes buttons that open a trapdoor, sending people to their deaths.) Before going to bed that evening, he uncrosses the eyes of the hunter/king in his portrait. Then he tours his collection of paintings, lusts after a sweet young shepherdess in one painting, and scowls at the dashing young chimney sweep in the neighboring painting. While he is asleep, the paintings come to life. The shepherdess and the chimney sweep declare their love for each other and decide to escape from their frames. As they are doing this, the hunter/king jumps from his painting to stop them. Neither he nor the statue of an old rider, who is supposed to guard over them, manage to prevent their escape. During the ruckus, the sleeping king awakes and cannot believe his eyes when he sees what the hunter/king is doing. However, the hunter/king uses the trapdoor in the floor to get rid of him forever and assumes his identity. The double replaces the original king, reminiscent of how the shadow replaces his master in Andersen's story "The Shadow."

With the entire palace on alert, the shepherdess and the chimney sweep, who marvel at the world outside and are enchanted to be free, are pursued by the royal police, portrayed as flying bats and devious thugs. Only the intervention of Mr. Bird can help them for a time, but they are finally captured along with the bird and locked up in a dark underworld that resembles an impoverished Paris inhabited by common people who are all forlorn. The plight of the masses is represented by a blind man, who plays magical music on an organ grinder. At one point, the king arrives on top of a giant metal robot and threatens to have the chimney sweep and the bird killed unless the shepherdess promises to marry him. She is forced to accept, and while she is taken from them, they are sent to a dungeon, where the organ grinder has managed to tame ferocious lions and tigers with his marvelous music. Now the bird uses the music and his own oratory skills to rouse the lions and tigers to rebel against the tyranny of the king.

The animals virtually storm the palace to interrupt the king's marriage with the shepherdess. The pompous wedding guests scatter. The king flees with the shepherdess to his humongous iron giant, but he is pursued by the shepherd, who attacks him. Meanwhile Mr. Bird takes control of the giant's levers and directs the machine's hand to pick up the king and toss him far into the wide universe. Immediately thereafter, the machine begins to destroy the entire city. In the final scene, the machine is sitting alone in the pose of Rodin's The Thinker. The bird's little son is once again caught in a diminutive cage — the naughty bird is always getting caught — and gently the hand of the iron giant reaches over, lifts the gate of the cage, and the little bird flies off into freedom.

Film critic Noel Megahey comments:

> "The animation is superb — beautifully designed sets and backgrounds full of technical marvels, wondrous caverns, towers, arches, Venetian canals and squares and vast palaces with Escher-like staircases. Each of the animators worked on their own characters, imbuing them with their own personality and characteristics — the king for example moves with the graceful fluidity of his creator, the chief animator Henri Lacam. Considering the amount of effort that went into acquiring a twenty year old film and the personal involvement that each of the creators put into the film, Le Roi et L'Oiseau is clearly a labor of love — and it shows. Rarely is animation so vital, so alive and so life-affirming — full of magic, wit, personality and imagination."[6]

Indeed, Le Roi et l'Oiseau is an improvement over the first cinematic version of 1952 (La Bergère et le ramoneur), which Grimault wanted to remake because he considered the film artistically flawed. During the early 1950s Grimault had financial problems and arguments with the producers that prevented him from finishing the film the way he desired, and he disowned the 1952 production. This is why he obtained the rights in 1976, gathered some of the former animators and new ones around him, and ordered a new musical score written by the Polish composer Wojciech Kilar. The result is a masterpiece, perhaps one of the most insightful critiques of Andersen's tale and an extraordinary demonstration of how fairy-tale animation can be used to address contemporary social and political issues.

The reason why Grimault and Prévert retitled the film as *The King and Mr. Bird* is because the film is no longer about the love between the shepherdess and the chimney sweep, but about the struggle between the small oppressed people, represented by the bird and his offspring, and the cruel dictatorial king. As Grimault himself said:

> The shepherdess and the chimney sweep, for example, are characters used as pretext: their very simple love will set off chain reactions. They are charming and nice, and everything that happens to them touches us. But it is the conflict between the king and the bird that gradually takes precedence. Moreover, it is the reason for changing the title of the film: *The Shepherdess and the Chimney Sweep* became *The King and Mr. Bird* — in regard to Andersen and the film *The Shepherdess and the Chimney Sweep*, the king and the bird assume much more importance. The bird, he represents liberty. He knows that the earth is round because he has taken a trip around it. What are borders for him? He doesn't care about them. He goes beyond them. He's at home everywhere. The only thing that he asks is that nobody harms his little ones. The king, he represents oppression: dictatorial, egotistical, megalomaniac, omnipotent.[7]

Clearly, Grimault and Prévert were influenced by the period of French and German fascism and were horrified by oppressive governments and the use of technology to intimidate people and cause mass destruction. Consequently, the tale in which Andersen reconfined his protagonists after they pursue freedom is transformed into a struggle for freedom and a transformation of technology to support the cause of freedom.

Ethics and Adaptation

The film adaptations of Andersen's tales raise some interesting ethical questions with regard to his legacy. For instance, is it ethical to produce a film that not only warps Andersen's intentions as a serious writer, but also overshadows his work and his life to such an extent that he and his tales are literally obfuscated and erased? This is certainly the case in such films as the *RKO Hans Christian Andersen* (1954) and the Disney *The Little Mermaid* (1989). But what has ethics to do with free artistic expression? Haven't artists always taken their material from the past, altered it, appropriated it, and reproduced it in keeping with their interests and the expectations of their audiences? Isn't such adaptation their prerogative and right? Is there a politically correct way to reproduce Andersen's stories for the cinema and TV? Can ethics lead to censorship?

I raise these questions because they are relevant for understanding the struggle over Andersen's legacy in English-speaking countries, especially the United States and the United Kingdom, and especially because they reflect upon the culture wars in America. The authenticity of art, which Andersen so valiantly and desperately sought to defend against the artificial and instrumental interests of the upper classes and intelligentsia in his own time, is in play when it comes to determining whether the misunderstood Andersen will ever have a chance to be understood. The difference between his day and our own is that his legacy, and hence the distinction between authentic and artificial art, is mediated through a powerful culture industry that marginalizes all serious endeavors to comprehend artworks and artists of the past and their historical significance. The culture industry not only participates in a public sphere in which critical discourse takes place, but it helps create it and sets the parameters of what can be discussed and distributed.

One of the more immoral tendencies within the American culture industry concerns the exploitation of children, children's needs, and children's expectations and the deception of the public at large fostered by films that pretend to speak truths and record history. Perhaps one should use the word "amorality" when referring to the culture industry because the corporations that control it are virtually without morals, and their bottom line for judging the quality of their films and TV shows is profit. Because the moral standards that the film industry and TV conglomerates pretend to uphold are so shallow and contradictory, and because even religion has become a commodity, there can be no question of ethics and morals in regard to the making of fairy-tale films, whether they be made for educational purposes or pure entertainment. The culture industry markets ethics and is immune to ethical questions that are bothersome like fleas. And yet, there still are and must be ethical questions, otherwise art itself would not be meaningful, and the humanities would be insignificant. In America, more than ever before, the culture wars call for ethical questions that challenge and judge the amoral assumptions of all culture producers, especially those who operate and hold power in the culture industry.

In Andersen's case, it is vital for the survival of culture that contemporary audiences gain a more palpable sense of how disturbed he was by social class discrimination and the rigid norms of propriety and religion of his own time. His disturbance should be our own. I say "should be" because there is a kind of moral imperative in culture that informs our humanity. We all want to be treated as we treat others, and to treat a writer and his works as if they were simply commodities and means to make profit can be considered immoral and unethical. There is something perverse in the fraudulent representation of the works and life of an artist who gave his life to art and to his people.

There cannot be a correct, ethical prescription of how to represent Andersen and his tales in film. Yet there are tendencies in the films that enable us to see how honest and serious the producers are with regard to Andersen's legacy. The more critical they are of Andersen and his works, in my opinion, the more they are just and creative in their own. The more they are disturbed by the very same things that disturbed Andersen, the more potential they have in passing on Andersen's legacy and remaining truthful to it. This is, I believe, the ethical responsibility of artists when they appropriate another artist's work.

I want to close by briefly discussing two examples of ethical and unethical appropriation in the fairy-tale film industry because they have a bearing on Andersen's legacy. One example, Michael Sporn's animated Andersen films, is directly related to Andersen's tales, and the second, *Finding Neverland* (2004), the live-action film about J. M. Barrie's life, is indirectly related to the portrayal of Andersen's life.

In 1990–92, Michael Sporn, an American animator, adapted three of Andersen's fairy tales, "The Nightingale," "The Red Shoes," and "The Little Match Girl" for Italtoons Corporation, and they are currently distributed by Weston Woods Studios, an educational company. The films, each about twenty-five minutes in length and created for children between five and ten, have been shown on HBO, but for the most part they have not received wide public attention, and thus they can be considered marginal cultural products of the culture industry. Their marginality is all the more reason that they deserve our attention, because Sporn's films, written by Maxine Fisher, are profound interpretations of Andersen's stories that transcend age designation and keep alive Andersen's legacy. They all use voice-over and colorful still sets as backdrops, and the animation uses naively ink-drawn characters who come alive because they are so unpretentious and resemble the simple and found art of children.

Two of Sporn's films are particularly important because they transform motifs from Andersen's tales to deal with contemporary social problems. Both take place in New York City, and the music and dialogue capture the rhythms and atmosphere of present-day urban life. In *The Red Shoes*, Sporn depicts the warm friendship of two little black girls, Lisa and Jenny, and how they almost drift apart because of a change in their economic situation. The story is narrated by Ozzie Davis as a shoemaker, who lives in a poor section of New York. Lisa and Jenny often visit him, and he describes their lives and how both love to dance and play and enjoy each other's company. One day Lisa's family wins the lottery, and they move to another part of the city. Now that she is rich, Lisa ignores Jenny until they meet at a ballet about the red shoes. The spoiled Lisa ignores Jenny, but later she returns to her own neighborhood and steals some red shoes that the shoemaker had been making for Jenny. Guilt-ridden, Lisa finds that the red shoes have magic and bring her back to the old neighborhood and help her restore her friendship with Jenny.

In *The Little Match Girl*, Sporn depicts a homeless girl, Angela, who sets out to sell matches on New Year's Eve 1999 to help her family living in an abandoned subway station on Eighteenth Street. She meets a stray dog named Albert, who becomes her companion, and together they try to sell matches in vain at Times Square. The night is bitter cold, and they withdraw to a vacant lot where Angela lights three matches. Each time she does this she has imaginary experiences that reveal how the rich neglect the poor and starving people in New York City. Nothing appears to help her, and when she tries to make her way back to the subway station, she gets caught in a snowstorm, and it seems that she is dead when people find her at Union Square the next morning. However, she miraculously recovers, thanks to Albert, and the rich people, gathered around her (all reminiscent of those in the dream episodes), begin to help her and her family.

Sporn's films are obviously much more uplifting than Andersen's original tales. But his optimism does not betray Andersen's original stories because of his moral and ethical concern in Andersen and his subject matter. Sporn's films enrich the tales with new artistic details that relate to the contemporary scene, and they critique them ideologically by focusing on the intrepid nature of the little girls rather than on the power of some divine spirit. At the same time, they are social comments on conditions of poverty in New York City that have specific meaning and can also be applied to the conditions of impoverished children throughout the world. What distinguishes Sporn's films from Andersen's stories is that he envisions a hope for change in the present, whereas Andersen promises rewards for suffering children in a heavenly paradise.

Sporn's films are tendentious in that they purposely pick up tendencies in Andersen's tales to express some of the same social concerns that Andersen wanted to address. His critical spirit is maintained, and even some of his faults are revealed. Most important, he is taken seriously. This cannot be said for the "immoral" work of Marc Forster in the film *Finding Neverland* (2004), based on Allen Knee's play. Though this film has been widely praised in the American media, it is, like the film *Hans Christian Andersen*, a good example of how a literary and personal legacy can be destroyed and twisted in a spectacle that creates a false illusion about the significance of a major English writer. I choose here to write about Barrie and not about Andersen because this new film is the most recent example of the unethical way some so-called writers of children's literature are presented in the public sphere — presented in such a way that thousands if not millions of viewers will come to accept the fictive Barrie as the real one.

Some brief facts: J. M. Barrie was a very short man, barely five feet tall, who became involved with the Llewelyn Davies family as early as 1897, when there were only three Davies boys aged four, three, and one. From the time of this meeting until the time of Sylvia Llewelyn Davies's death in 1910, Barrie intruded into the Davies's affairs so much so that Sylvia's husband Arthur resented him and tried to keep him out. But Barrie persisted until they were both dead, and he became the foster father of the boys more by force than by the will of Sylvia. His play, *Peter Pan, or the Boy Who Would Not Grow Up,* was never intended for children, and it always had the backing of the American producer Charles Frohman. There were no children from the children's hospital at the first performance. Barrie, who was impotent, had a very strange relationship with the Davies boys that bordered on pedophilia.

In *Finding Neverland,* all these facts are twisted into a tear-jerking love story between Sylvia and Barrie, who are played by celebrity stars Kate Winslet and Johnny Depp. Instead of the troubled, intrusive Barrie, the film depicts a noble, dedicated, sensitive writer, whose wife and Sylvia's mother mistreat and misunderstand. Poor chaste Barrie must live down the suspicions of society. He dotes on the boys and Sylvia because he simply cares for them. There is not the slightest lascivious or lustful sign in Depp's portrayal of Barrie. It is as if he were sexless and as if the love he shared with Sylvia, if there was such a love, was totally innocent. Yet, we know that Barrie was a very calculating and manipulative individual. His play was never performed in Sylvia's parlor in 1904 when she and her husband were very much alive, and Peter Davies, the eldest son, who supposedly became the man of the family, grew up to hold Barrie in contempt.

What are we to make of the romantic portrait of Barrie in Forster's film and Knee's play? Certainly, they have a right, as all artists do, to sweeten, change, alter, and remake an artist and his work.[8] But it is clear that they have done Barrie and themselves a disservice by not treating him with more critical care according to a more faithful account of history. An embellished Barrie is an ugly Barrie, as is the case in the depiction of Andersen in *Hans Christian Andersen*. Indeed, the handsome Barrie becomes more listless and boring in their treatment, for he was a very troubled writer, difficult to portray because of his mood swings, just like Hans Christian Andersen, whose legacy does not need to be turned into a myth. On the contrary, the myths and fairy tales spread about Barrie deserve to be questioned so that we can grasp how and why it is he came to produce works that have caught our imagination and still play an enormous role in Western culture.

This is also true of Andersen, which is why I have drawn a comparison with Barrie. If we recall his image in the *RKO film Hans Christian Andersen*, it is practically impossible to catch a glimpse of who Andersen was and why he wrote. His history was for the most part repressed by the film, which superficially treats the trials and tribulations of his life. His legacy can be better sensed in the film adaptations of his works. But here, too, only traces of Andersen's original impetus can be found in the films based on his tales over the past fifty years. Fortunately, the field of cultural production is still open enough that there are competing versions of what his work means and how his life should be played out. Given the significance of the mass media in the twenty-first century, especially of film, let us hope that his legacy will not succumb to immoral trivialization. After all, Andersen knew and strongly represented a viewpoint that we should never forget: the making of art poses an ethical problem.

Endnotes

Preface

1. Letter to Kirstine Marie Iversen on 4 January 1837. Quoted in Niels Kofoed, "Hans Christian Andersen and the European Tradition," in *Hans Christian Andersen: Danish Writer and Citizen of the World,* ed. Sven Rossel (Amsterdam: Rodopi, 1996), 233.

2. Viggo Hjørnager Pedersen, *Ugly Ducklings? Studies in the English Translations of Hans Christian Andersen's Tales and Stories* (Odense: University of Southern Denmark, 2004), 16.

Chapter 1: In Pursuit of Fame: an Introduction to the Life and Works of Hans Christian Andersen

1. There is a split image of Andersen between scholars and the general public in the United States and the United Kingdom. Ever since the publication of Elias Bredsdorff's superb biography, *Hans Christian Andersen: The Story of His Life and Work, 1805–75* (London: Phaidon, 1975), critics and specialists have been familiar with the sad facts of Andersen's life and his diverse production as a writer. However, the general public has very little notion of his complex character. As Diane Crone Frank and Jeffrey Frank have recently written in their highly informative introduction to the translation of his tales, "beyond Scandinavia Andersen has generally been regarded not as a literary genius but as a quaint nineteenth-century writer of charming stories. Nothing contributed more to this view than *Hans Christian Andersen,* the 1952 Danny Kaye film. Although it had almost nothing to do with the real Andersen — and, to be fair, never claimed to — the movie helped to make an idealized version of the writer's life as familiar as his fairy tales, almost an extension of them" (*The Stories of Hans Christian Andersen* [Boston: Houghton Mifflin, 2003], 2–3). Jackie Wullschlager's thorough biography, *Hans Christian Andersen: The Life of a Storyteller* (London: Penguin, 2000), has also revealed how troubled a person Andersen was, although she spends much too much time trying to prove his homosexuality, something denied by Bredsdorff and the Franks. One need only read Andersen's tales to see the dark side of his rosy public image that the mass media and popular culture have created. By far the most comprehensive and insightful biography is by Jens Andersen, *Andersen–En Biografi,* 2 vols. (Copenhagen: Gyldendal, 2003). This work has appeared in German, and an English edition is in preparation. Aside from being the most reliable biography, Andersen (no relation) provides a full

picture of the writer's friends, cities, and social conditions and demonstrates that Hans Christian Andersen was a shrewd businessman who superbly promoted all his works.

2. Hans Christian Andersen, *Das Märchen meines Lebens ohne Dichtung* (Leipzig: Lorek, 1847), 1–2.

3. Elias Bredsdorff, *Hans Christian Andersen: The Story of His Life and Work, 1805–75* (London: Phaidon, 1975), 16.

4. *Ibid.*, 54.

5. *The Diaries of Hans Christian Andersen*, ed. Patricia Conroy and Sven Rossel (Seattle: University of Washington Press, 1990), 8.

6. *Aus Andersens Tagebüchern*, vol. 1, ed. and trans. Heinz Barüske, (Frankfurt am Main: Fischer, 1980), 34–5.

7. *The Diaries of Hans Christian Andersen*, 59.

8. Diana Crone Frank and Jeffrey Frank, "The Real H. C. Andersen," in *The Stories of Hans Christian Andersen*, trans. and ed. Diane Crone Frank and Jeffrey Frank (Boston: Houghton Mifflin, 2003), 11.

9. The Franks have an excellent account of Andersen's relationship with Jette Wulff and his desire to travel to America. See "The Real H. C. Andersen," 19–36. Another important essay on this topic is Erik Dal's "Hans Christian Andersen's Tales and America," *Scandinavian Studies* 40 (1968): 1–25.

10. Søren Kierkegaard, *From the Papers of One Still Living*, in *The Essential Kierkegaard*, ed. Howard V. Hong and Edna H. Hong (Princeton, N.J.: Princeton University Press, 2000), 13–19.

11. Hans Christian Andersen, *O. T.: A Danish Romance* (Boston: Houghton, Osgood, 1880), 1.

12. Georg Brandes, "Hans Christian Andersen," in *Eminent Authors of the Nineteenth Century*, trans. R. B. Anderson (New York: Crowell 1886), 104–5.

13. Heinrich Teschner, "Hans Christian Andersen und Heinrich Heine: Ihre literarischen und persönlichen Beziehungen" (Ph.D. diss., University of Münster: Westfällische Vereinsdruckerei, 1914), 189.

14. Niels Kofoed, "Hans Christian Andersen and the European Literary Tradition," in *Hans Christian Andersen: Danish Writer and Citizen of the World*, ed. Sven Rossel (Amsterdam: Rodopi, 1996), 213.

15. W. Glyn Jones, *Denmark* (New York: Praeger, 1970), 66–7. See also Kofoed, "Hans Christian Andersen and the European Literary Tradition," 216–7.

16. Johan de Mylius, "Hans Christian Andersen and the Music World," in *Hans Christian Andersen: Danish Writer and Citizen of the World*, ed. Sven Rossel (Amsterdam: Rodopi, 1996), 176–208.

17. Frederick Marker, *Hans Christian Andersen and the Romantic Theater: A Study of Stage Practices in the Prenaturalistic Scandinavian Theater* (Toronto: University of Toronto Press, 1971), 31.

18. *The Diaries of Hans Christian Andersen*, 137–8.

19. Hans Christian Andersen, *Pictures of Sweden*, trans. Charles Beckwith (London: Bentley, 1851), 321–2, 323.

20. Hans Christian Ørsted, *The Soul in Nature*, trans. Leonora Horner and Joanna Horner (London: Bohn, 1852), 128.

21. Hans Christian Andersen, *Das Märchen meines Lebens ohne Dichtung*, trans. Michael Birkenbihl (Frankfurt am Main: Insel, 1979), 145–6.

22. Actually, Andersen wrote more than 156 tales, and they can be found in the standard edition of his works. Some were published in his travel books, others in magazines. Some were rough drafts in letters and papers discovered after his death. The last official publication of his stories, however, contained 156 tales.

23. For a thorough and informative account of English translations of Andersen's works, see Viggo Hjørnager Pedersen, *Ugly Ducklings? Studies in the English Translations of*

Hans Christian Andersen's Tales and Stories (Odense: University Press of Southern Denmark, 2004).

24. Like the Brothers Grimm, Andersen never wrote exclusively for children. His primary concern was to have success among adult readers, which is the case today in Europe and North America. As the public and market for children's literature grew in the nineteenth century, his tales were printed in editions or picture books designed especially for children. This publishing strategy continued into the twentieth century, but the tales selected for children are generally very limited. The majority of Andersen's writings continued to be read primarily by adults, and even today in the United States, Andersen's fairy tales are taught at universities, and his works are mainly appreciated by students, librarians, teachers, and professors.

25. For a full discussion of this topic, see Bengt Holbek's important essay, "Hans Christian Andersen's Use of Folktales," in *A Companion to the Fairy Tale,* ed. Hilda Ellis Davidson and Anna Chaudri (Cambridge: D.S. Brewer, 2003), 149–58.

26. Mathias Winther, *Danish Folk Tales,* 1823, trans. T. Sands and J. Massengale (Madison, Wis.: Wisconsin Introductions to Scandinavia, 1989).

27. Jack Zipes, *The Brothers Grimm: From Enchanted Forests to the Modern World* (New York: Routledge, 1988), 54–7.

28. Hans Christian Andersen, *The Complete Fairy Tales and Stories,* trans. Erik Christian Haugaard (New York: Doubleday, 1974), 1. Note that all quotations from the fairy tales are taken from this edition, and the page references in the text refer to the Haugaard translation.

29. Poul Houe, "Going Places: Hans Christian Andersen, the Great European Traveler," in *Hans Christian Andersen: Danish Writer and Citizen of the World,* ed. Sven Rossel (Amsterdam: Rodopi, 1996), 123–75.

30. In Danish, Andersen uses the term lærde mand or "learned man," which can be translated as either philosopher or scholar. But such a man can also be interpreted as the traditional poet, who does not write poetry out of emotion but slavishly follows the rules of classical forms. Therefore, the so-called classical poetry of truth, beauty, and good is regarded by Andersen as divorced from poetic inspiration. From this perspective, the learned man is a slave to dead values, and the shadow is a manipulative destroyer of this slave and has no values at all. Genuine poetry, which stems from inspiration and is a force of life, is absent in this pessimistic story that reveals how traditionalism can turn on itself and bring about its own destruction.

31. Clayton Koelb, *Inventions of Reading: Rhetoric and the Literary Imagination* (Ithaca, N.Y.: Cornell University Press, 1988), 219.

Chapter 2: The Discourse of the Dominated

1. Heinrich Teschner, "Hans Christian Andersen und Heinrich Heine: Ihre literarischen und persönlichen Beziehungen" (Ph.D. diss., University of Münster: Westfälische Vereinesdruckerei, 1914), 189. "Er kam mir vor, wie ein Schneider; er sieht auch wirklich ganz so aus. Er ist ein hagerer Mann mit einem hohlen, eingefallenen Gesichte und verrät in seinem äußeren Anstande ein ängstliches, devotes Benehmen, so wie die Fürsten es gern lieben. Daher hat Andersen auch bei allen Fürsten eine so glänzende Aufnahme gefunden. Er repräsentiert vollkommen die Dichter wie die Fürsten sie gern haben wollen."

2. Niels Kofoed, "Hans Christian Andersen and the European Literary Tradition," in *Hans Christian Andersen: Danish Writer and Citizen of the World* (Amsterdam: Rodopi, 1996), 216–7.

3. Elias Bredsdorff, *Hans Christian Andersen: The Story of His Life and Work* (London: Phaidon, 1975), 152.

4. Ibid., 179. Many more statements like this can be found in Andersen's letters and diaries. See *Hans Christian Andersen's Correspondence with the Late Grand-Duke of Saxe-Weimar, Charles Dickens, etc.*, ed. Frederick Crawford (London: Deen & Son, 1891); *The Diaries of Hans Christian Andersen*, ed. Patricia Conroy and Sven Rossel (Seattle: University of Washington Press, 1990); *Das Märchen meines Lebens. Briefe. Tagebücher*, ed. Erling Nielsen (Munich: Winkler, 1961); *Aus Andersens Tagebüchern*, ed. Heinz Barüske, 2 vols. (Frankfurt am Main: Fischer, 1980).

5. Ibid., 132–3.

6. Noëlle Bisseret, *Education, Class Language and Ideology* (London: Routledge & Kegan Paul, 1979), 1–2.

7. See Jeffrey M. Blum, *Pseudoscience and Mental Ability* (New York: Monthly Review Press, 1978) and Stephan L. Chorover, *From Genesis to Genocide: The Meaning of Human Nature and the Power of Behavior Control* (Cambridge: MIT Press, 1979).

8. For the general development in Europe, see Jürgen Habermas, *Strukturwandel der Öffentlichkeit. Untersuchungen zu einer Kategorie der bürgerlichen Gesellschaft* (Neuwied: Luchterhand, 1962) and Charles Morazé, *The Triumph of the Middle Classes. A Political and Social History of Europe in the Nineteenth Century* (London: Weidenfeld and Nicolson, 1966). For Denmark, see W. Glyn Jones, *Denmark* (New York: Praeger, 1968).

9. Michel Foucault, *Discipline and Punish* (New York: Pantheon, 1968).

10. Bisseret, *Education, Class Language and Ideology*, 26.

11. Bredsdorff, *Hans Christian Andersen*, 54.

12. Ibid., 69.

13. Cf. *The Fairy Tale of My Life*, trans. W. Glyn Jones (New York: British Book Centre, 1955). Andersen wrote three autobiographies during his life, and each one is filled with distortions and embellishments of his life.

14. Jones, *Denmark*, 66–67.

15. Cf. Paul V. Rubow, "Idea and Form in Hans Christian Andersen's Fairy Tales," in *A Book on the Danish Writer Hans Christian Andersen*, ed. Sven Dahl and H. G. Topsøe-Jensen (Copenhagen: Det Berlingske Bogtrykkeri, 1955), 97–136.

16. Bisseret, *Education, Class Language and Ideology*, 63–4.

17. Ibid., 65.

18. Bengt Holbek, "Hans Christian Andersen's Use of Folktales," in *A Companion to the Fairy Tale*, ed. Hilda Ellis Davidson and Anna Chaudri (Cambridge: D. S. Brewer, 2003), 153.

19. Finn Hauberg Mortensen, *A Tale of Tales: Hans Christian Andersen and Children's Literature*, Parts III and IV (Minneapolis: Center for Nordic Studies, University of Minnesota, 1989), 16–7.

20. See Lutz Röhrich, "Dankbarer Toter (AaTh 505–508)," in *Enzyklopädie des Märchens*, ed. Kurt Ranke, Vol. 3 (Berlin: De Gruyter, 1999), 306–22.

21. Antti Aarne and Stith Thompson, *The Types of the Folktale*, 2nd rev. ed. (Helsinki: Suomalainen Tiedeaktatemia, 1991), 171–5.

22. Holbek, "Hans Christian Andersen's Use of Folktales," 155.

Chapter 3: The Discourse of Rage and Revenge: Controlling Children

1. See Flemming Mouritsen, "Children's Literature," in *A History of Danish Literature*, ed. Sven Rossel (Lincoln: University of Nebraska Press, 1992), 609–31. Whereas Mouritsen praises Andersen for transcending the norms of children's literature during this period, I believe that Andersen was much more conservative and conventional than most Andersen scholars admit. Certainly his writing style and themes were unusual for his time, but the ideological and didactic uses of children in his tales are very much in keeping with traditional Christian thinking of the nineteenth century.

2.   Finn Hauberg Mortensen, *A Tale of Tales: Hans Christian Andersen and Danish Children's Literature*, Parts I and II (Minneapolis: Center for Nordic Studies, University of Minnesota, 1989), 44.

3.   Although it is difficult to schematize which texts are "child-centered," the following tales about children reveal a great deal about Andersen's views regarding children: "The Naughty Boy," "The Storks," "The Little Mermaid," "The Ugly Duckling," "The Bronze Pig," "The Angel," "The Red Shoes," "The Little Match Girl," "Grief," "Little Tuck," "The Snow Queen," "Five Peas from the Same Pod," "Ib and Little Christina," "The Girl Who Stepped on Bread," "Children's Prattle," "The Dead Child," "In the Children's Room," and "What the Whole Family Said."

4.   Adam Phillips, *The Beast in the Nursery: On Curiosity and Other Appetites* (New York: Pantheon, 1998), xv.

5.   Ibid., 56.

6.   Ibid., 123.

7.   Ibid., 126.

8.   Hans Christian Andersen, *The Complete Fairy Tales and Stories*, trans. Erik Christian Haugaard (New York: Doubleday, 1974), 39. Note that all quotations from the fairy tales are taken from this edition, and the page references in the text refer to the Haugaard translation.

9.   Ibid., 39.

10.   Erin Mackie "Red Shoes and Bloody Stumps," in *Footnotes: On Shoes*, ed. Shari Benstock and Suzanne Ferriss (New Brunswick, N.J.: Rutgers University Press, 2001), 233–47.

11.   Ibid., 235.

12.   See ""Hyacinth and Roseblossom," in *Spells of Enchantment: The Wondrous Fairy Tales of Western Culture*, ed. Jack Zipes (New York: Viking, 1991), 300–3.

13.   W. Glyn Jones, "Andersen and Those of Other Faiths," in Hans Christian Andersen: *A Poet in Time*, ed. Johan de Mylius, Aage Jørgensen, and Viggo Hjørnager Pedersen (Odense: Odense University Press, 1999), 259–70.

14.   Jacqueline Rose, *The Case of Peter Pan or The Impossibility of Children's Fiction*, 2nd ed. (Philadelphia: University of Pennsylvania Press, 1991), 3–4.

15.   Ibid., 4.

Chapter 4: The Cinematic Appropriation of Andersen's Heritage: Trivialization and Innovation

1.   James Massengale, "The Miracle and A Miracle in the Life of a Mermaid," in *Hans Christian Andersen: A Poet in Time*, ed. Johann de Mylius, Aage Jørgensen, and Viggo Hjørnager Pedersen (Odense: Odense University Press, 1999), 555.

2.   *Hans Christian Andersen, The Complete Fairy Tales and Stories*, trans. Erik Haugaard (New York: Doubleday, 1974), 66. Note that all quotations from the fairy tales are taken from this edition, and the page references in the text refer to the Haugaard translation.

3.   See Roberta Trites, "Disney's Sub/version of The Little Mermaid," *Journal of Popular Television and Film* 18 (1990/91): 145–59.

4.   Laura Sells, "'Where Do the Mermaids Stand?' Voice and Body in The Little Mermaid," in *From Mouse to Mermaid: The Politics of Film, Gender, and Culture*, eds. Elizabeth Bell, Lynda Haas, Laura Sells (Bloomington: Indiana University Press, 1995), 185.

5.   This film was dubbed into English with the voices of the British actors Peter Ustinov, Denholm Elliott, Claire Bloom, and Max Adrian. Unfortunately, it has not had a wide distribution in the United States and is not well known, even though it has had a strong influence on the successful Japanese animator Hayao Miyazaki.

6. Noel Megahey, "Le Roi et L'Oiseau"; available on-line at http://www.dvdtimes.co.uk/content.php?contentid=6335. Last accessed March 31, 2005.

7. Jean-Pierre Pagliano, *Paul Grimault*, 2nd ed. (Paris: Dreamland, 1996), 56. "La Bergère et le Ramoneur, par exemple, sont des personnages pretextes dont l'amour tout simple va déclencher des reactions en chaîne. Il sonts charmants, gentils, tout ce qui leur arrive nous touche, mais c'est le conflit entre le Roi et l'Oiseau qui prend progressivement la première place. C'est d'ailleurs la raison du changement de titre du film: La Bergère et le Ramoneur est devenu Le Roi et l'Oiseau — le Roi et l'Oiseau ont pris beaucoup plus d'importance, par rapport à Andersen et par rapport au film La Bergère et le Ramoneur. L'Oiseau, c'est la liberté. Il sait que la terre est ronde parce que'il en a fait le tour. Qu'est-ce-que c'est les frontières pour lui? Il s'enfout, il passe au-dessus. Il est partout chez lui. La seule chose qu'il demand, c'est qu'on n'emmerde pas ses petits. Le Roi, c'est l'oppression: dictatorial, égoïste, mégalomane, tout puissant."

8. For an interesting review of Finding Neverland, which more or less defends the film as a good "weepie," see Anthony Lane, "Lost Boys: Why J. M. Barrie Created Peter Pan," *The New Yorker*, 22 November 2004, 98–103. Although Lane recognizes that there may be huge distortions in the film, when he remarks that "Depp [the actor playing J. M. Barrie] resembles Barrie in no way, except in his slenderness of form," he completely avoids the ethical question of such a misleading and sentimental portrait of the writer, even when he calls Barrie a wounded creature whose works are painful to read.

Bibliography

Original Works by HCA

Autobiography

H. C. Andersens Levnedsbog. Copenhagen: 1805–1831. Edited by Hans Brix. Copenhagen: Aschehoug, 1926.
Das Märchen meines Lebens ohne Dichtung. Leipzig: Lorck, 1847.
Mit Livs Eventyr. Copenhagen: Reitzel, 1855.
Das Märchen meines Lebens. Briefe. Tagebücher, ed. Erling Nielsen. Munich:Winkler, 1969.

Selected Dramas

Ungdoms-Forsøg (Youthful attempts). Copenhagen: Schorelin, 1822.
Kjaerlighed paa Nicolai Taarn (Love on St. Nicholas Tower). Copenhagen: Reitzel, 1829.
Den Unsynglige paa Sprogø (The invisible man on Sprogfø). Copenhagen: Reitzel, 1839.
Mulatten (The Mulatto). Copenhagen: Reitzel, 1840.
Fugelen i Paeretraeet (The Bird in the Pear Tree). Copenhagen: Reitzel, 1842.
Lykkens Blomst (The Blossom of Happiness). Copenhagen: Reitzel 1845.
Meer end Perler og Guld (More than Pearls and Gold). Copenhagen: Reitzel, 1849.

Librettos

Festen paa Kenilworth (The Festival at Kenilworth, 1836). Copenhagen: Samfundet til Udgivelse af Dansk Musik, 1877.
Agnete og Havmanden (Agnete and the Merman). 1843. First published as a dramatic poem. Copenhagen: Luno & Schneider, 134.
Liden Kirsten (Little Christina). Copenhagen: Lose & Delbanco, 1846.

Poetry

Digte (Poems). Copenhagen: Hagerup, 1830.
Phantasier og Skizzer (Fantasies and Sketches). Copenhagen: 1831.
Kjendte og glemte digte, 1823–1867. Copenhagen: Reitzel, 1867.

Novels

Improvisatoren (The Improvisatore). Copenhagen: Reitzel, 1835.
O. T. Copenhagen: Reitzel, 1836.
Kun en Spillemand (Only a Fiddler). Copenhagen: Reitzel, 1837.
De to Baronesser (The Two Baronesses). Copenhagen: Reitzel, 1848.
At være eller ikke være (To Be or Not to Be?). Copenhagen: Reitzel, 1857.
Lykke-Peer (Lucky Peter). Copenhagen: Reitzel, 1870.

Stories

Eventyr fortalte for Børn (Fairy Tales Told for Children). Copenhagen: Reitzel, 1835.
Nye Eventyr (New Fairy Tales). Copenhagen: Reitzel, 1843.
H. C. Andersens Eventyr: Kritisk udgivet efter de originale Eventyrhæfter med Varianter (H. C. Andersen's Fairy Tales). Edited by Erik Dal, Erling Nielsen, and Flemming Hovmann. Copenhagen: Reitzel, 1963–1990.

Travel

Fodrejse fra Holmens Kanal til Østpynten of Amager i Aarene 1828 og 1829 (Journey on Foot from Holmens Canal to the East Point of Amager). 1829.
En Digters Bazar (A Poet's Bazaar). Copenhagen: Reitzel, 1842.
I Sverige (In Sweden). Copenhagen: Reitzel, 1851.
I Spanien (In Spain). Copenhagen: Reitzel, 1863.
Et besøg i Portugal (A Visit to Portugal). Copenhagen: 1868.

Translations

Collections of Andersen's Fairy Tales
Wonderful Stories for Children. Translated by Mary Howitt. London: Chapman and Hall, 1846.
The Complete Stories of Hans Christian Andersen. Edited and Translated by Jean Hersholt. 3 vols. New York: Heritage Press, 1942.
Hans Christian Andersen's Fairy Tales. Translated by R. P. Keigwin. With an introduction by Elias Bredsdorff. New York, 1950.
The Complete Fairy Tales and Stories. Translated by Erik Christian Haugaard. New York: Doubleday, 1974.
Tales and Stories by Hans Christian Andersen. Translated by Patricia Conroy and Sven Rossel. Seattle: University of Washington Press, 1980.
The Stories of Hans Christian Andersen. Translated by Diane Crone Frank and Jeffrey Frank. Boston: Houghton Mifflin, 2003.
Fairy Tales. Translated by Tiina Nunnally. Edited by Jackie Wullschlager. New York: Viking, 2004.

Other Works

Andersen's Works. 10 vols. Author's ed. Boston: Houghton, Osgood, 1869–1871.
The Andersen-Scudder Letters. Edited and translated by Waldemar Westergaard. With an introduction by Jean Hersholt and an essay by Helge Topsøe-Jensen. Berkeley CA: University of California Press, 1949.
Aus Andersens Tagebüchern. Edited and translated by Heinz Barüske. 2 vols. Frankfurt am Main: Fischer, 1980.

Brothers, Very Far Away and Other Poems. Edited by Sven Rossel. Seattle: Mermaid Press, 1991.

The Diaries of Hans Christian Andersen. Edited and translated by Patricia Conroy and Sven Rossel. Seattle: University of Washington Press, 1990.

The Fairy Tale of My Life. Translated by W. Glyn Jones. New York: British Book Center, 1954.

The Fairy Tale of My Life. Translated by Horace Scudder. New York: Hurd and Houghton, 1868.

Hans Christian Andersen's Correspondence with the Late Grand-Duke of Saxe Weimar, Charles Dickens, etc. Edited by Frederick Crawford. London: Deen & Son, 1891.

In Spain. Translated by Mrs. Bush. London: Bentley, 1864.

In Spain, and a Visit to Portugal. New York: Hurd and Houghton, 1871.

In Sweden. Translated by Mrs. Bushby. London: Routledge, 1852.

The Improvisatore; or, Life in Italy. Translated by Mary Howitt. 2 vols. London: Bentley, 1845.

Lucky Peter. Translated by Horace E. Scudder. *Scribner's Monthly*, March and April 1871.

Das Märchen meines Lebens ohne Dichtung. Translated by Michael Birkenbihl. Frankfurt am Main: Insel, 1979.

Only a Fiddler. Translated by Mary Howitt. London: Bentley, 1845.

Pictures of Sweden. Translated by Charles Beckwith. London: Bentley, 1851.

Pictures of Travel in Sweden, among the Hartz Mountains, and in Switzerland, with a Visit at Charles Dickens' House. New York: Hurd and Houghton, 1871.

A Poet's Bazaar. Translated by Charles Beckwith. 3 vols. London: Bentley, 1846.

Rambles in the Romantic Regions of the Hartz Mountains. Translated by Charles Beckwith. London: Bentley, 1848.

Seven Poems. Translated by R. P. Keigwin. Odense: Hans Christian Andersen's House, 1955.

The Story of My Life. Translated by Horace E. Scudder. Boston: Hurd and Houghton, 1871.

To Be or Not to Be? Translated by Mrs. Bush. London: Bentley, 1857.

The True Story of My Life. Translated by Mary Howitt. London: Longman, Brown, Green, and Longmans, 1847.

The Two Baronesses. Translated by Charles Beckwith. 2 vols. London: Bentley, 1848.

A Visit to Portugal 1866. Translated and edited by Grace Thornton. London: Peter Owen, 1972.

A Visit to Spain. Translated and edited by Grace Thornton. London: Peter Owen, 1975.

Critical Works

Aarne, Antti and Stith Thompson. *The Types of the Folktale*, 2nd rev. ed. Helsinki: Suomalainen Tiedeakatemia, 1991.

Atkins, A. M. "The Triumph of Criticism: Levels of Meaning in Hans Christian Andersen's The Steadfast Tin Soldier." *Scholia Satyrica* 1 (1975): 25–8.

Andersen, Jens. *Andersen–En Biografi*. 2 vols. Copenhagen: Gyldendal, 2003; German translation, *Hans Christian Andersen: Eine Biographie*. Translated by Ulrich Sonnenberg. Frankfurt am Main: Insel, 2005.

Bain, R. Nisbet. *Hans Christian Andersen: A Biography*. New York: Dodd, Mead, 1895.

Barilske, Heinz. "Hans Christian Andersen — Der Mensch und seine Zeit." In *Aus Andersens Tagebüchern*. Vol. 1. Frankfurt am Main: Insel, 1980.

Bartmann, Christoph. "Die Grosse Verkaufe." *Literaturen* 3 (2005): 16–17.

Bell, Elizabeth, Lynda Haas, and Laura Sells, eds. *From Mouse to Mermaid: The Politics of Film, Gender, and Culture*. Bloomington: Indiana University Press, 1995.

Berendsohn, Walter A. *Phantasie und Wirklichkeit in den "Märchen und Geschichten" Hans Christian Andersens: Struktur- und Stilstudien*. Wiesbaden: Sändig, 1973.

Berger, Eberhard and Joachim Giera, eds. *77 Märchenfilme: Ein Filmführer für jung und alt*. Berlin: Henschel, 1990.

Bisseret, Noëlle. *Education, Class Language and Ideology*. London: Routleage & Keagan Paul, 1979.

Böök, Fredrik. *Hans Christian Andersen: A Biography*. Translated by G. Schoolfield. Norman: University of Oklahoma Press, 1962.

Born, Ann. "Hans Christian Andersen: An Infectious Genius." *Anderseniana* 2 (1976): 248–60.

Brandes, Georg. "Hans Christian Andersen." In *Eminent Authors of the Nineteenth Century*. Translated by R. B. Anderson. New York: Crowell, 1886.

Braude, L. Y. "Hans Christian Andersen and Russia." *Scandinavica* 14 (1975): 1–15.

Bredsdorff, Elias. *Hans Andersen and Charles Dickens: A Friendship and Its Dissolution*. Copenhagen: Rosenkilde and Bagger, 1956.

———. *Hans Christian Andersen: The Story of His Life and Work, 1805–75*. London: Phaidon, 1975.

Bredsdorff, Thomas. *Deconstructing Hans Christian Andersen: Some of His Fairy Tales in the Light of Literary Theory — and Vice Versa*. Minneapolis: Center for Nordic Studies, University of Minnesota, 1993.

Browning, George. *A Few Personal Recollections of Hans Christian Andersen*. London: Unwin, 1875.

Burnett, Constance B. *The Shoemaker's Son: The Life of Hans Christian Andersen*. New York: Random House, 1941.

Dahlerup, Pil. "Splash! Six Views of "The Little Mermaid." *Scandinavian Studies* 63, 2 (1991): 141–63.

Dal, Erik. "Hans Christian Andersen's Tales and America." *Scandinavian Studies* 40 (1968): 1–25.

Detering, Heinrich. "Der Welt-Narziss." *Literaturen* 3 (2005): 7–15.

Duffy, Maureen. "The Brothers Grimm and Sister Andersen." In *The Erotic World of Faery*. London: Hodder and Stoughton, 1972.

Frank, Diane Crone and Jeffrey Frank. "A Melancholy Dane." *The New Yorker*, 8 January 2001, 78–84.

———. "The Real Hans Christian Andersen." In *The Stories of Hans Christian Andersen*. Translated by Diane Crone Frank and Jeffrey Frank. Boston: Houghton Mifflin, 2003.

Godden, Rumer. *Hans Christian Andersen: A Great Life in Brief*. New York: Knopf, 1955.

Grant, John. *Masters of Animation*. New York: Watson-Guptill, 2001.

Grønbech, Bo. *Hans Christian Andersen*. Boston: Twayne, 1980.

Grundtvig, N. F. S. *Selected Writings*, Edited by Johannes Knudsen. Philadelphia: Fortress Press, 1976.

Haugaard, Erik C. "Hans Christian Andersen: A Twentieth-Century View." *Scandinavian Review* 14 (1975): 1–15.

Hees, Annelies van. "The Little Mermaid." In *H. C. Andersen: Old Problems and New Readings*. Edited by Steven Sondrup. Provo, Utah: Hans Christian Andersen Center, Brigham Young University; University of Southern Denmark Press, 2004.

Heltoft, Kjeld. *Hans Christian Andersen as an Artist*. Translated by Reginald Spink. Copenhagen: Royal Danish Ministry of Foreign Affairs, 1977.

Holbek, Bengt. "Hans Christian Andersen's Use of Folktales." In *A Companion to the Fairy Tale*. Edited by Hilda Ellis Davidson and Anna Chaudri. Cambridge: D.S. Brewer, 2003.

Houe, Poul. "Going Places: Hans Christian Andersen, the Great European Traveler." In *Hans Christian Andersen: Danish Writer and Citizen of the World*. Edited by Sven Rossel. Amsterdam: Rodopi, 1996.

———. "Andersen in Time and Place — Time and Place in Andersen." In *Hans Christian Andersen: A Poet in Time*. Edited by Johan de Mylius, Aage Jørgensen, and Viggo Hjørnager Pedersen. Odense: Odense University Press, 1999.

Jan, Isabelle. *Andersen et ses contes: Essai*. Paris: Aubier, 1977.

Johnson, Spencer. *The Value of Fantasy: The Story of Hans Christian Andersen*. La Jolla, Calif.: Value Communications, 1979.

Jones, W. Glyn. *Denmark*. New York: Praeger, 1970.

———. "Andersen and Those of Other Faiths." In *Hans Christian Andersen: A Poet in Time*. Edited by Johan de Mylius, Aage Jørgensen, and Viggo Hjørnager Pedersen. Odense: Odense University Press, 1999.

Jørgensen, Aage. *Hans Christian Andersen through the European Looking Glass*. Odense: Odense University Press, 1998.

Kierkegaard, Søren. *The Essential Kierkegaard*. Edited by Howard V. Hong and Edna H. Hong. Princeton, N.J.: Princeton University Press, 2000.

Koelb, Clayton. *Inventions of Reading: Rhetoric and the Literary Imagination*. Ithaca, N.Y.: Cornell University Press, 1988.

Kofoed, Niels. "Hans Christian Andersen and the European Literary Tradition." In *Hans Christian Andersen: Danish Writer and Citizen of the World*. Edited by Sven Rossel. Amsterdam: Rodopi, 1996.

Lane, Anthony, "Lost Boys: Why J. M. Barrie Created Peter Pan." *The New Yorker*, 22 November 2004, 98–103.

Lederer, Wolfgang. *The Kiss of the Snow Queen: Hans Christian Andersen and Man's Redemption by Women*. Berkeley: University of California Press, 1986.

Maar, Michael. "Andersens Nachleben." In Hans Christian Andersen. *Schräge Märchen*. Trans. Heinrich Detering. Munich: Deutscher Taschenbuch Verlag, 2002. Pp. 284–98.

Macho, Thomas. "Wem gehören die Märchen." *Literaturen* 3 (2005): 18–25.

Manning-Sanders, Ruth. *Swan of Denmark: The Story of Hans Christian Andersen*. London: Heinemann, 1949.

Marker, Frederick. *Hans Christian Andersen and the Romantic Theater: A Study of Stage Practices in the Prenaturalistic Scandinavian Theater*. Toronto: University of Toronto Press, 1971.

Massengale, James. "The Miracle and a Miracle in the Life of a Mermaid." In *Hans Christian Andersen: A Poet in Time*. Edited by Johan de Mylius, Aage Jørgensen, and Viggo Hjørnager Pedersen. Odense: Odense University Press, 1999.

Meynell, Esther. *The Story of Hans Andersen*. New York: Schuman, 1950.

Mishler, William, "H. C. Andersen's 'Tin Soldier' in a Freudian Perspective." *Scandinavian Studies* 50 (1978): 389–95.

Mitchell, P. M. *A History of Danish Literature*. Copenhagen: Gyldendal, 1957.

Mortensen, Finn Hauberg. *A Tale of Tales: Hans Christian Andersen and Danish Children's Literature*. Parts I–IV. Minneapolis: Center for Nordic Studies, University of Minnesota, 1989.

Mouritsen, Flemming. "Children's Literature." In *A History of Danish Literature*. Edited by Sven Rossel. Lincoln: University of Nebraska Press, 1992.

Mudrick, Marvin. "The Ugly Duck." *Scandinavian Review* 68 (1980): 34–48.

Murphy, Patrick. "'The Whole Wide World Was Scrubbed Clean': The Androcentric Animation of Denatured Disney." In *From Mouse to Mermaid: The Politics of Film, Gender and Culture*, Edited by Elizabeth Bell, Lynda Haas, and Laura Sells. Bloomington: Indiana University Press, 1995.

Mylius, Johan de. *The Voice of Nature in Hans Christian Andersen's Fairy Tales*. Odense: Odense University Press, 1989.

———. "Hans Christian Andersen and the Music World." *In Hans Christian Andersen: Danish Writer and Citizen of the World*. Edited by Sven Rossel. Amsterdam: Rodopi, 1996.

Mylius, Johan de, Aage Jørgensen, and Viggo Hjørnager Pedersen, eds. *Hans Christian Andersen: A Poet in Time*. Odense: Odense University Press, 1999.

Nielsen, Erling. *Hans Christian Andersen in Selbstzeugnissen und Bilddokumenten*. Hamburg: Rowohlt, 1958.

———. *Hans Christian Andersen (1805–1875): The Writer Everybody Reads and Loves, and Nobody Knows*. Copenhagen: Royal Danish Ministry of Foreign Affairs, 1983.

Ørsted, Hans Christian. *The Soul in Nature*. Translated by Leonora Horner and Joanna Horner. London: Bohn, 1852.

Pagliano, Jean-Pierre. *Paul Grimault*. Paris: Dreamland, 1996.

Pedersen, Viggo Hjørnager. *Ugly Ducklings? Studies in the English Translations of Hans Christian Andersen's Tales and Stories*. Odense: University Press of Southern Denmark, 2004.

Phillips, Adam. *The Beast in the Nursery: On Curiosity and Other Appetites*. New York: Pantheon, 1998.

Prince, Alison. *Hans Christian Andersen: The Fan Dancer*. London: Allison & Busby, 1998.

Ranke, Kurt, ed. *Enzyklopädie des Märchens*. 12 vols. Berlin: De Gruyter, 1979–2005.

Reumert, Elith. *Hans Christian Andersen the Man*. Translated by Jessie Brochner. London: Reumert, 1927.

Robb, N. A. "Hans Christian Andersen." In *Four in Exile*. Port Washington, NY: Kennikat Press, 1948, 1968.

Röhrich, Lutz. "Dankbarer Toter (AaTh 505–508)." In *Enzyklopädie des Märchens*. Edited by Kurt Ranke. Vol. 3. Berlin: De Gruyter, 1999.

Rose, Jacqueline. *The Case of Peter Pan or The Impossibility of Children's Fiction*. 2nd ed. Philadelphia: University of Pennsylvania Press, 1992.

Rossel, Sven, ed. *A History of Danish Literature*. Lincoln: University of Nebraska Press, 1992.

———. ed. *Hans Christian Andersen: Danish Writer and Citizen of the World*. Amsterdam: Rodopi, 1996.

———. *Hans Christian Andersen und seine Märchen heute*. Vienna: Picus, 1996.

Rubow, Paul V. "Idea and Form in Hans Christian Andersen's Fairy Tales." In *A Book on the Danish Writer Hans Christian Andersen: His Life and Work*. Copenhagen: The Committee for Danish Cultural Activities Abroad, 1955.

Sells, Laura. "'Where Do the Mermaids Stand?' Voice and Body in The Little Mermaid." In *From Mouse to Mermaid: The Politics of Film, Gender, and Culture*. Edited by Elizabeth Bell, Lynda Haas, and Laura Sells. Bloomington: Indiana University Press, 1995.

Solomon, Charles. *Enchanted Drawings: The History of Animation*. rev. ed. New York: Wings Books, 1994.

Sondrup, Steven, ed. *H. C. Andersen: Old Problems and New Readings*. Provo, Utah: Hans Christian Andersen Center, Brigham Young University: University of Southern Denmark Press, 2004.

Special issue on Hans Christian Andersen. *Études Germaniques* 58, 4 (2003). With contributions by Marc Auchet, Johan de Mylius, Peer E. Sørensen, Poul Houe, Niels Kofoed, Frank Hugus, Annelies van Hees, Sven Hakon Rossel, and Heinrich Detering.

Spink, Reginald. *Hans Christian Andersen and His World*. London: Thames & Hudson, 1972.

Stirling, Monica. *The Wild Swan: The Life and Times of Hans Christian Andersen*. London: Collins, 1965.

Svendsen, Hanne Marie and Werner Svendsen. *Geschichte der dänischen Literatur*. Neumünster: Wachholtz, 1964.

Teschner, Heinrich. "Hans Christian Andersen und Heinrich Heine: Ihre literarischen und persönlichen Beziehungen." Ph.D. diss., University of Münster, 1914.

Toksvig, Signe. *The Life of Hans Christian Andersen*. London: Macmillan, 1933.

Trites, Roberta. "Disney's Sub/version of The Little Mermaid." *Journal of Popular Television and Film* 18 (1990/91): 145–59.

Winther, Mathias. *Danish Folk Tales*. 1823. Translated by T. Sands and J. Massengale. Madison: Wisconsin Introductions to Scandinavia, 1989.

Wullschlager, Jackie. *Hans Christian Andersen: The Life of a Storyteller*. London: Penguin, 2000.

———. "Introduction to Hans Christian Andersen." *Fairy Tales*. Translated by Tiina Nunnally. Edited by Jackie Wullschlager. New York: Viking, 2004.

Zipes, Jack. *Fairy Tales and the Art of Subversion: The Classical Genre for Children and the Process of Civilization*. London: Heinemann, 1983.
———. "Hans Christian Andersen." In *European Writers: The Romantic Century*. Vol. 6. Edited by J. Jacques Barzun. New York: Scribner's, 1985.
———. *The Brothers Grimm: From Enchanted Forests to the Modern World*. New York: Routledge, 1988.

Film Bibliography[1]

Hans Christian Andersen (1954)
    United States, color, 112 minutes
        Director: Charles Vidor
        Screenplay: Moss Hart
        Words and music: Frank Loesser
        Studio: Samuel Goldwyn
        Cast: Danny Kaye (Hans Christian Andersen),
            Farley Granger, Zizi Jeanmaire

The Emperor's New Clothes (1953)
    United States, color, animation
        Director: Ted Parmelee
        Screenplay: Robinson MacLean
        Voices: Hans Conreid (various voices)

The Emperor's New Clothes (1972)
    United States, color, live action, cell animation, 51 minutes
        Director: Arthur Rankin and Jules Bass
        Screenplay: Romeo Muller
        Music: Maury Laws
        Lyrics: Jules Bass
        Producer: Arthur Rankin and Jules Bass

---

[1] In some cases I was not able to obtain complete information about certain films. However, I have made every effort to provide the basic references.

Studio: ABC (network special)
Cast: Danny Kaye (Narrator)
Voices: Danny Kaye (Marmaduke), Cyril Ritchard (Emperor Klonkenlocker), Imogene Coca (Princess Klonkenlocker), Alan Swift (Musty), Robert McFadden (Jaspar)

The Emperor's New Clothes (1985)
United States, color, 54 minutes
Director: Peter Medak
Screenplay: Mark Curtiss and Rod Ash
Producers: Bridget Terry and Frederick Fuchs
Executive producer: Shelley Duvall
Cast: Alan Arkin (Bo), Art Carney (Morty), Georgia Brown (Maggie), Dick Shawn (Emperor)

The Emperor's New Clothes (1987)
United States/Israel, color, 85 minutes
Director: David Irving
Screenplay: David Irving, Anna Mathias, and Len Talan
Music: David Krivoshi
Songs: Stephen Lawrence
Lyrics: Michael Korie
Camera: David Gurfinkel
Studio: Cannon
Cast: Sid Caesar (Emperor), Robert Morse (Henry Spencer), Jason Carter (Nicholas Spencer), Lysette Anthony (Princess Gilda), Clive Revill (Prime Minister), Julian Joy Chagrin (Duke), Danny Segev (Prince Nino)

The Emperor's New Clothes (1997)
United States, color, animation, 30 minutes
Director: Robert Van Nutt
Screenplay: Eric Metaxas
Music: Mark Isham
Illustration: Robert Van Nutt
Producer: Mark Sottnick and Mike Pogue
Studio: Rabbit Ears
Voices: John Gielgud (Narrator)

The Emperor's New Clothes (1993; *Cisarovysaty,* 1993;
  Des Kaisers neue Kleider, 1994)
  Czechoslovakia/Germany, color, 87 minutes
    Director: Juraj Herz
    Screenplay: Bernd Fiedler
    Cast: Harald Juhnke (Emperor), Andréa Ferréol (Duchess),
      Jan Kalous (Tobias), Carsten Voigt (Lorenzo), Therese
      Herz (Maria), Andrei Hryc (Major), Juraj Herz (Plafond),
      Milos Nesvadba (Master of Ceremonies), Radek Kuchar
      (Tschako)

The Emperor's New Clothes (1995)
  United States, color, animation, 26 minutes
    Director: Bruce Smith and Edward Bell
    Studio: Sony Wonder (HappilyEver After: Fairy Tales for
      Every Child)
    Voices: Robert Guillaume (Narrator), George Takei,
      Gedde Watanabe

Cisaruv slavík (*The Emperor's Nightingale,* 1948)
  Czechoslovakia, color, live-action/animated, 73 minutes
    Director: Jiri Trnka and Jiri Brdecka (animation)
    Director: Milos Makovec (live-action scenes)
    Screenplay: Jiri Trnka and Jiri Brdecka
    Music: Vaclav Trojan
    Camera: Ferdinand Pecenka
    Cast: Boris Karloff (Narrator), Helena Patockova (Girl),
      Jaromir Sobotoa (Boy)
  English language version: *The Emperor's Nightingale* (1951)
    Runtime: 60 minutes
    Screenplay: Phyllis McGinley
    Producer: William S. Snyder
    Studio: Rembrandt Films
    Voices: Boris Karloff (Narrator)

La Petite marchande d'alumettes (*The Little Match Girl,* 1928)
  France, black and white, 29 minutes
    Director: Jean Renoir

The Little Match Girl (1999)
  United States, color, animation, 30 minutes
    Director: Michael Sporn
    Screenplay: Maxine Fisher
    Music: Caleb Sampson
    Camera: Gary Becker
    Animation: Steven Dovas, Ray Kosarin, Theresa Smythe, and
      Michael Sporn
    Executive producer: Giuliana Nicodemi
    Studio: Family Home Entertainment, Italtoons Corp.
    Voices: F. Murray Abraham (Narrator), Perry Kiefer
      (Jazzman), Theresa Smythe (Angela), Heidi Stallings
      (Aunt Fritzi Ritz)

Hans Christian Andersen's The Little Mermaid (1975)
  Japan, color, animation, 74 minutes
    Director: Tomoharu Katsumata and Tim Redi
    Screenplay: Mieko Koyamauchi
    Voices: Richard Chamberlain (Narrator), Fumie Kashiyama
      (Marina), Mariko Miyagi (Fritz the Dolphin), Taro Shigaki
      (Prince), Hideki Shibata (Mermaid King), Kousei Tomita
      (Duke the Shark), Kaneta Kimotsuki (Crab/Conch),
      Ichirô Nagai (Whistler), Kenichi Ogata (Oval Shark),
      Haruko Kitahama (Witch), Miyoko Azabu (Mermaid Crone)

Malá morská víla (*The Little Mermaid*, 1975)
  Czechoslovakia, color, 104 minutes
    Director: Karel Kachyna
    Screenplay: Ota Hofman
    Cast: Miroslava Safránková (Little Mermaid), Radovan
      Lukavský (King of All Seas), Petr Svojtka (Prince of
      the Southern Empire), Libuse Safránková (Princess),
      Marie Rosulková (Mermaid's Grandmother),
      Milena Dvorská (Sorceress)

Rusalochka (*The Little Mermaid*, 1976)
  Russia, color, 81 minutes
    Director: Vladimir Bychkov
    Screenplay: Victor Viktovich and Grigory Yagufeld

Camera: Emil Vagenstein
Music: Yevgheny Krylatov
Studio: Gorky Film Studio
Cast: Viktoriya Novikova (Sorceress or Witch)
 Valentin Nikulin (Sulpitius), Galina Artyomova (Princess),
 Yuri Senkevich (Prince), Galina Volchek (Mermaid),
 Stefan Iliyev (Ritzar), Mikhail Pugovkin (Ribak)

La Petite sirène (*The Little Mermaid*, 1980)
 France, color, 105 minutes
 Director: Roger Andrieux
 Screenplay: Roger Andrieux and Yves Dangerfield
 Cast: Philppe Léotard (Georges Maréchal), Laura Alexis
 (Isabelle Pélissier), Evelyne Dress (Nelly), Mare Dubois
 (Benédicte Pélissier), Marianne Winquist (Véronique),
 Diane Sorelle (Claire)

The Little Mermaid (1984)
 United States, color, 55 minutes
 Director: Robert Iscove
 Screenplay: Anne Beatts
 Producer: Shelley Duvall
 Cast: Karen Black (Sea Witch), Brian Dennehy
 (King Neptune), Pam Dawber (Pearl), Helen Mirren

The Little Mermaid (1989)
 United States, color, animation, 83 minutes
 Director: Ron Clements and John Musker
 Screenplay: Roger Allers
 Songs: Howard Ashman and Alan Menken
 Studio: Disney
 Voices: Jodi Benson (Ariel), Christopher Daniel Barnes
 (Eric), Pat Carroll (Ursula), Jason Marin (Flounder),
 Samuel Wright (Sebastian), Kenneth Mars (Triton),
 Buddy Hackett (Scuttle)

The Little Mermaid (1992–94)
 United States, color, animation, TV series, 30 minutes, 31 episodes
 Director: Jamie Mitchel

Studio: Disney
Voices: Jodie Benson (Ariel), Samuel Wright (Sebastian),
    Mary Kay Bergman (Arista), Sheryl Bernstein (Acquata),
    Pat Carroll (Ursula), Danny Cooksey (Urchin),
    Edan Gross (Flounder), Maurice LaMarche (Scuttle),
    Kenneth Mars (Triton)

The Little Mermaid II: Return to the Sea (2000)
    United States, color, animation, 75 minutes
        Director: Jim Kammerud and Brian Smith
        Screenplay: Elizabeth Anderson and Temple Mathews
        Studio: Disney
        Voices: Jodi Benson (Ariel), Samuel Wright (Sebastian),
            Tara Strong (Melody), Pat Carroll (Morgana),
            Buddy Hackett (Scuttle), Kenneth Mars (Triton),
            Max Casella (Tip), Stepen Furst (Dash), Rob Paulsen (Eric),
            Cam Clarke (Flounder), Rene Auberjonois (Louis),
            Kay Kuter (Grimsby)

The Nightingale (1983)
    United States, color, 50 minutes
        Director: Ivan Passer
        Producer: Shelley Duvall
        Cast: Mick Jagger (Emperor), Bud Cort (Music Master),
            Babara Hershey (Kitchen Maid), Edward James Olmos
            (Prime Minister), Shelley Duvall (Narrator)

Nightingale (1999)
    United States, color, animation, 25 minutes
        Director: Michael Sporn
        Screenplay: Maxine Fisher
        Music: Caleb Sampson
        Camera: Gary Becker
        Animation: Sue Perrotto and Michael Sporn
        Executive producer: Giuliana Nicodemi
        Studio: Family Home Entertainment, Italtoons Corp.
        Voices: Mako (Narrator), June Angela (Girl)

Printsessa na goroshine (*The Princess and the Pea*, 1976)
Russia, color, 89 minutes
    Director: Boris Rytsarev
    Screenplay: Felix Mironer
    Camera: Vyacheslav Yegorov
    Music: Based on the works of Antonio Vivaldi
    Studio: Gorky Film Studio
    Cast: Irina Malysheva, Andrei Podoshyan,
        Innokenty Smoktunovsky, Alissa Freindlikh,
        Irina Yurevich, Marina Livanova, Svetlana Orlova

The Princess and the Pea (1983)
United States, color, 50 minutes
    Director: Tony Bill
    Screenplay: Mark Curtis and Rod Ash
    Producer: Shelley Duvall
    Cast: Beatrice Straught (Queen Veronica), Nancy Allen
        (Princess Elizabeth), Pat McCormick (King Frederick),
        Liza Minelli (Princess Alicia), Tom Conti (Prince Richard),
        Tim Kazurinsky (The Fool)

Die Prinzessin und der Schweinehirt (*The Princess and the Swineherd*, 1953)
West Germany, black and white, 82 minutes
    Director: Herbert B. Fredersdorf
    Screenplay: Emil Surmann
    Producer: Friedrich Kurth
    Cast: Dieter Ansbach (Prince Honestheart), Liane Croon
        (Princess Rosemouth), Isle Furstenburg, Victor Janson,
        Harry Wustenhagen
English language version: The Princess and the Swineherd (1968)
    Director: Reuben Guberman
    Producer: K. Gordon Murray
    Associate producer: Sheldon Schermer
    Editor: J. R. Demy

The Red Shoes (1948)
United Kingdom, color, 133 minutes
    Director: Michael Powell and Emeric Pressburger

Screenplay: Michael Powell
Music: Brian Easdale
Camera: Jack Cardiff
Producers: George Busby, Michael Powell, and Emeric
Pressburger
Studio: Rank
Cast: Anton Walbrook (Boris Lermontov), Marius Goring
(Julian Craster), Moira Shearer (Victoria Page),
Robert Helpmann (Ivan Boleslawsky), Léonide Massine
(Grischa Ljubov), Albert Basserman (S. Ratov),
Ludmilla Tchérina (Irina), Esmond Knight (Livingstone)

The Red Shoes (1983)
United States, color, 79 minutes
Director: John Clark Donahue and John Driver
Studio: Children's Theatre Company (Minneapolis),
Television Theatre Co.
Cast: Rana Haugen (Karen Sorenson), Stephen Boe
(Hans Christian Andersen), Molly Atwood
(Mrs. Ingrid Sorenson), Julee Cruise (Old Rag Face),
Wendy Lahr (Old Lady), Myron Johnson (Shoemaker),
Carl Beck (Soldier), George Muschamp (Preacher)

The Red Shoes (1990)
United States, color, animation, 27 minutes
Director: Michael Sporn
Screenplay: Maxine Fisher
Music: Caleb Sampson
Producer: Michael Sporn
Executive producer: Giuliana Nicodemi
Studio: Family Home Entertainment, Italtoons Corp.
Animation: Tissa David, Doug Compton, Yvette Kaplan, and
Michael Sporn
Voices: Ossie Davis

La Bergère et le ramoneur (*The Shepherdess and the Chimney
Sweep*, 1950)
France, Technicolor, animation, 64 minutes

Director: Paul Grimault
Screenplay: Jacques Prévert and Paul Grimault
Music: Joseph Kosma
Producer: Joseph Kosnic
Voices: Peter Ustinov (Mr. Wonderbird), Claire Bloom
(Shepherdess)
English language version: *The Curious Adventures of
Mr. Wonderbird* (1952)

Le Roi et l'Oiseau (*The King and Mr. Bird*, 1979)
France, Eastman color, animation, 87 minutes
Director: Paul Grimault
Screenplay: Jacques Prévert and Paul Grimault
Music: Wojciech Kilar
Studio: Les Films Paul Grimault-Les Films Gibé-Antenne 2
Voices: Jean Martin (Mr. Bird), Pascal Mazzotti (King),
Raymond Bussières (Chief of Police), Agnès Viala
(Shepherdess), Renaud Marx (Chimney Sweep),
Roger Blin (Blind Man)

The Snow Queen (*Snezhnaya Koroleva*, 1957)
USSR (Russia), color, animation, 55 minutes
Director: Lev Atamanov
Screenplay: Lev Atamanov, Nikolai Erdman
Art Direction: Leonid Shvartsman, Aleksandr Vinokurov
Production: Soyuzmultifilm
English Language Version: 1959
Unversal International, 74 minutes
Director: Phil Patton
Producer: Richard Patton
Screenplay: Alan Lipscott, Bob Fisher
Music: Frank Skinner
Songs: Diane Lampert, Richard Loring
Cast: Art Linkletter, Tammy Marthoch, Jennie Lynn,
Billy Booth, Rickey Busch
Voices: Sandra Dee (Gerda), Timmy Kirk (Kay), Patty
McCormick (Angel), Louise Arthur (Snow Queen),
Lillian Buyeff (Granny)

The Snow Queen (*Snezhnaya Koroleva*, 1966)
   USSR (Russia), color, 85 minutes
      Director: Gennadi Kazansky
      Screenplay: Yevgheny Schwartz
      Cast: Nikolai Boyarksy, Irina Gubanova, Natalya Klimova,
         Andres Kostrichkin, Yevgeniya Melinkova

The Snow Queen (1995)
   United Kingdom, color, animation, 75 minutes
      Director: Martin Gates
      Screenplay: Sue Radley, Martin Gates
      Production: Martin Gates in Association with Carrington
         Productions International
      Voices: Ellie Beaven, David Jason, Hugh Laurie, Rik Mayall,
         Julia McKenzie, Helen Mirren, Imelda Staunton

The Snow Queen (*Snedonnigen*, 2000)
   Denmark, color, 26 minutes
      Directors: Jacob Jørgensen and Kristof Kuncewicz
      Screenplay: Margrethe II
      Cast: Christian Elmelund (Kay), Ronja Mannov (Gerda),
         Margrethe II (narrator, Esther Knudsen)

The Snow Queen (2202)
   USA, made for Television, color, 180 minutes
      Director: David Wu
      Teleplay: Simon Moore
      Cast: Bridget Fonda (Snow Queen), Jeremy Guilbaut (Kai),
         Chelsea Hobbs (Gerda), Robert Wisden (Wolfgang),
         Meghan Black (Robber Girl)

Index